Best Poets of 2019

Vol. 2

John T. Eber Sr.
MANAGING EDITOR

A publication of

Eber & Wein Publishing
Pennsylvania

Best Poets of 2019: Vol. 2
Copyright © 2020 by Eber & Wein Publishing as a compilation.

Rights to individual poems reside with the artist themselves. This collection of poetry contains works submitted to the publisher by individual authors who confirm that the work is their original creation. Based upon the author's confirmations and to that of the Publisher's actual knowledge, these poems were written by the listed poets. Eber & Wein, Inc. does not guarantee or assume responsibility for verifying the authorship of each work.

The views expressed within certain poems contained in this anthology do not necessarily reflect the views of the editors or staff of Eber & Wein Publishing.

All rights reserved under the International and Pan-American copyright conventions. No part of this book may be reproduced, stored in a retrieval system, or transmitted in any form, electronic, mechanical, or by other means, without written permission of the publisher. Address all inquires to Rachel Eber, 50 E. High St., New Freedom, PA 17349.

Library of Congress
Cataloging in Publication Data

ISBN 978-1-60880-670-6

Proudly manufactured in the United States of America by

Eber & Wein Publishing
Pennsylvania

A note from the editor

> "We are half-survivors
> Cast up upon these shores"
> *from* "Refuge" (page 1)

When we began accepting poems for this series last September, little did any of us know the crisis we would find ourselves amidst come March 2020. When ninety-eight-year-old Irene Backalenick, once a writer for the *New York Times*, wrote her poem "Refuge" last year, little did she know that her sentiments *then* would take on a prophecy of their own when *now*, less than a year later, nursing homes and assisted living facilities across the nation would account for the majority of sicknesses and deaths throughout a nationwide (and global) pandemic. Little did she know that hospitals in every state would become "wreckage" sites for thousands of "half-survivors" and those not even that lucky.

In 2019, the care and compassion given by first responders, nurses, and medical staff had a profound impact on Irene's life as well as many lives of those sequestered in nursing homes. Today, the dedication and selflessness exuding from this group is having a profound impact on the world and on the lives of patients of all ages. The "brittle," depleted, hopeless scene Irene eloquently illustrates through metaphor has become a static scene on the news every day of the week. For now beaches will remain closed and "lifeless," but one thing is certain: like Irene and her fellow half-survivors, we will emerge from this crisis a "new-formed world" and all because of the refuge lovingly and unceasingly provided by medical professionals from coast to coast.

I hope for many this volume offers a brief reprieve from the monotony of quarantine life. The mind, however, can never be contained; therefore, keep it nourished by continuing to write.

Be well,
John Eber Sr.

Refuge

We are half-survivors
Cast up upon these shores
Twisted shards of wreckage
Maimed and broken, addled, dazed
Like brittle wall-eyed fish
Abandoned here at low tide
Or half-empty lifeless shells
No longer mollusk homes

But, wait, in this ungiving scene
Arise the first responders
These nurses, aides, and staffers
Building new sandcastles
With certainty, compassion
With soft and caring hands
Dedicated, educated, goal-driven
Daily thus a new-formed world
And this unlikely wreckage
Turns once again to life

Irene Margolis Backalenick
Bridgeport, CT

I was a working journalist for years, writing for The New York Times and other national publications. In my sixties, I acquired PhD in theater history and turned to theater criticism, a career I then pursued for some thirty years. When I moved to this senior facility in my nineties, I found a new genre—poetry. My poem "Refuge," written recently at age ninety-eight, was inspired by Watermark, the facility where I live.

In the Garden

My thoughts and dreams haunt me
of memories past working and pulling weeds
alongside my eighty-nine-year-old dad,
at times watering and loosening roots.
Gardening and mulching, his passion roses.
Newly-planted rosebushes next to fig trees
at the side of the house.
Alongside the driveway were also fig trees in a row.
Between his lips cigar smoke billowed,
filling the air with a layered cigar smoke fog.
Pulling weeds, spreading mulch, watering
an aura of gladness between us . . .
when I was not playing tennis with friends or my sister.
The air cool, sun beaming at us,
he turned and smiled at me.
Sunlight loosens mulch dirt and
growing rosebushes rooted pods of water—
a healthy nature coloring yard.
Peach and fig trees surround the house with beauty.
Baby roses Dad snips diagonally off the bush.
New growth roses decorate our wooden, claw-footed
seven-foot long hall table for dining and Sunday
brunch visitors.
Verbal sighs from visitors, eyes brighten, and lips
smile at roses beautifully centered in a crystal glass
vase that could be seen outside through the front
glass paneled door.

Alyx Jen
Dallas, TX

Our Friendly and Beautiful Kentucky Home

Mom, Dad, Brother Jim, dogs, and I happily
lived on South Main Street in Corbin, Kentucky,
in a friendly old pink house surrounded by a large yard
with a morning glory filled field on the south side
along with poplar and pine trees on the north side.
Our front door faced west toward the main highway
with cordial neighbors, sidewalks, pine hills beyond.
And downtown, South Ward School beckons to the north
as evergreen bushes and petunias bordered our house
and catalpa trees hugged the north and south sides.
With driveway and garage outside our bedroom's side door
the east back door led to the backyard patio and fireplace.
Irises, roses, and apple trees lined a path to the shed,
which sat along rocks and ferns by our tall back fence.
As my brother Jim and I played horse, touch football,
or walked downtown and had fun with our friends
at the Dime Store, Hippodrome movie, and snack shops,
Mom and Dad entertained "Elicon" work friends
at home in our kitchen, living room, or den.
As our dogs played by their doghouses in the backyard
near shady catalpas and the colorful morning glory trellis,
trains whizzed by on tracks behind the east back fence
at our friendly home in beautiful Corbin, Kentucky.

William D. Irwin
Princeton, IL

We dedicate this poem to our father (who was very proud of his family). He taught his children right from wrong, to be very hardworking, and to always keep their word. He worked hard to provide a better life for all of us and we love and thank him very much as we stand tall as men. We also dedicate this poem to our love of Kentucky. Kentucky is very beautiful and we're proud to have lived there.

Fields of Life

Fields of harvest, fields of toil.
Harvests of happiness grow out of the soil.

Fields of youth, fields of age.
Harvest the fruit, become a sage.

Virginia McCoy
Marina Del Ray, CA

Thoughts Do Overwhelm

After a fire, many years ago
the piles of the house's content
lay moldering in October's rainy flow
until my shocked brain could straighten its bends.

That evening was nothing, I now know,
since nature has shown its overwhelming disaster
wrecking nearly half our country with a fearsome blow
while showing human frailty so poorly bandaged as with only plaster.

Scattered talks of money, elections, and such, this past fall
now seems so very pathetic.
Perhaps, from unknown nature, there was a wake-up call.
And, perhaps, we should take heed of events all prophetic.

Helen-Anne Keith
Chelsea, MA

Seventy-Four Birthdays and Counting

A special time to celebrate,
a milestone to be shared
by those who care about others.
Living and loving each moment
and day in time can seem like a lifetime.
Thank God it is good, wonderful,
the absolute best of all things to happen.

It is always possible if you want it
to be the best life can offer.
An offering is a gift of beauty and joy
at any time, place, or moment. *Always.*

Annual events, personal to each individual
for that beginning of life,
something shared by each other,
both alone and together.

A birthday is special, unique,
individual, yet universal; we all have one
and deserve to love and enjoy
our moment with others.

Mine has been so blessed
because of those who share my world.
From the first moment until now,
I have had the distinct pleasure
of being a part of others
and bringing them to me.

Virginia Bowman EdD
Oakley, CA

Every birthday is significant but approaching seventy-five felt incredibly potent to me. Three quarters of a century was a landmark moment in my life, and it made me conscious of all I had experienced and what was left to come. I cherish the beauty that has gone before me and gratefully look forward to the time still remaining in the future. Being able to share all my joy is what has brought me to this moment. Hopefully those who read this message will be able to appreciate who they are and what they may also enjoy.

Paint for Me

Paint for me
A country church,
Peacefully tucked away,
From incessant noise
And needless strife,
A place where I can stay.

Paint for me
A watermelon,
Bright and sweet and gay.
A slice of childhood happiness
Cut fresh and new each day.

Paint for me
A sea-oat shore,
Where daring gulls fly free.
Where sand and sky, and such as I,
Look toward eternity.

Paint for me
Each time you paint,
Behind each stroke, I bless
The hand that speaks,
The heart that sings,
The soul I hear expressed.

Dianne T. Evans
Lancaster, SC

For Gail Plyler Hyatt

I Wasn't Ready for Love

I wasn't ready to be in love;
I didn't know that I wasn't whole.
I wasn't ready to fall in love,
but you came along and you touched my soul.

I thought that love was a special thing,
a state of being that came only once.
I thought that love would come when I was ready,
but you came and showed me what love was.

I wasn't ready when love came to me,
but every day I keep learning more
so that now I am ready for love at last
and I will be able to love you more.

Joel B. Belland
Kiel, WI

Arbol

Splendid, quiet, patient friend
High towering branches sky out to utmost end
A tremendous bouquet of leaves doth life keep in hold
Limbs tall and bushy, spreading out their fold
The birds will come. Homely place for all their young
Cool winds pass through, searching throughout its boughs
Deeply-rooted for its sways, no fall it seeks to know
And the noisy woodpecker has left his name in holes.
The colors are a gift of autumn; growth is of the rain
Strong, withstanding, crinkled wood made plain
Powerful, destructive, standing in domain
A proud landmark does stay
Loyal with its shade
Wise, old vine
Holding out a lifetime

Geisha Battle
Chester, VA

Five Senses

Out of all of my senses I would never want to lose my sight of eyes
Mainly because I would go insane
If I could never again see the morning sunlight
Shine off your beautiful face as it begins to rise
Even though I would hate not being able to taste your lips
Or being able to feel the touch of your hips
The smell of your hair fresh out of the shower
The sound of your voice especially your laughter
I would miss every second of every hour
I wouldn't be able to watch you use my chest
As your pillow while you sleep
I wouldn't be able to see your body
Wrapped around me warmer than any blanket could keep
I'd miss watching you jog the beach in the sand
I'd miss watching you try on clothes and lingerie brand after brand
I'd miss your goofy silly dances when you bite your food
I'd miss watching you without you even noticing
My eyes glued on you in the mood
Most importantly I would miss seeing my favorite sight I love
Even blind though your face, sunshine
Would always remain in my mind
Where nothing and no one could ever get rid of

Westley Louis Powell Jr.
Daly City, CA

My name is Westley Louis Powell Jr. My mother dearest and dad blessed me with a big family of four sisters and one brother. Music, poetry, and sports are my favorite hobbies. Always remember to live each day to the fullest. God is good all the time. Never stop believing in yourself or your dreams. I was inspired to write this poem thanks to a beautiful smart strong woman whom I call my sunshine.

Door to Heaven

Have faith, love and hope, no matter what,
Storms in life will pass, wherever we're at.
Walk in faith. even if that's all we got,
He will see us through, believe it or not.

Life is fleeting, life is bitter and sweet,
At times hard to forgive, hard to forget.
But we are forgiven, as we learn to forgive,
So keep an open heart, follow what Jesus said.

There are many doors as we walk through,
Some doors are wide, others are narrow.
We are set free to choose which door to follow,
So seek wisdom, thread with care as you go.

At times we blindly walk, we fail and stumble,
Seek and hold His hand, lest you will fall.
We may not realize, He is always there,
Ask, cry out His name and He will appear.

When we trust Jesus with all our hearts,
Heaven's door will open filled with bright lights.
Walk in, as heavenly music fills the air,
Pray no need to fear, He is constantly there.

Virgilia A. Smith
Marshall, MI

I am a "casual" ED RN from Marshall, MI, with two adult children. I wrote my first poem, "So, Just Believe" after my husband of thirty-three years died of lung cancer in 2009. It is also the title of my memoir. I have been writing poetry for a few years. My seven poems are published. I am lyricist of twelve songs. I wrote "Door to Heaven" one early morning when I could not go back to sleep. I have been to nineteen countries. Last year I taught Hawaiian dance at the senior center. I feel very blessed. Praise the Lord.

A Blessing to Be Free

A circus each day can be
With never-ending clowns.
Misguided frolicking free,
Their prison may get you down.

With never-ending clowns
Tugging at emotions,
Prison may produce frowns,
Enduring their notions.

Tugging at emotions,
Booted from place to place,
Prison may produce frowns.
No smile upon the face.

Booted from place to place,
Tied up with things to solve.
No smile upon the face,
'Til released to revolve.

Tied up with things to solve
From a circus that can be.
But released to revolve
Is a blessing to be free.

B. J. Boal
Des Moines, IA

May Belle

A lady of royalty descent
walks past me with grace.
Sways with the nimbleness of a swan,
splendid, magnificent, grand!
Hair as dark as the night
it flips, it frolics, it bounce.
Shines in the luster of the gloom
softly whispering breeze in dark sojourn.
Dainty brightly colored flower
gleefully traverse the prime of life.
Contend humanity's tempest storms,
serenity deep-seated in innermost soul.
Delicate she might be,
reflections of frailty.
Hidden strength is deeply laden
down innermost core of her being.
An oak standing in the midst
of weeds and the riotous wild,
unwavering, strong, and unbended,
God's hands of love forever shielded!

Adelfa G. Lorilla
Seagoville, TX

This poem is written for my daughter May Belle. This is a reflection of who she is, how she is, and what she is in real life. To us, her family, she is a real treasure, a very precious gift, and one of the eight blessings from God. We thank God for my husband Ricardo Lorilla, our children—Frances Karen, Jan Rex, Zheena May, Andrei James, Armi Grace, May Belle, Ricardo Jr., and Jesse Rey—children-in-law, and grandchildren. To God be the glory.

Day by Day

Aurora's dawn, arriviste, chroma rich!
The Harp and Artist beget the grande scene,
Whilst night sky pearls resplendently bewitch!

Homeless relegated to gentry's kitsch
Stone dwellings shelter box-tent homes 'tween.
Aurora's dawn, arriviste, chroma rich!

Children enslaved on a pirate keth.
Ungodly intent so evil, mean.
Whilst night sky pearls resplendently bewitch!

Thoughtless human rubble, a peccant glitch,
Fetid trash heaps defile the sphere, blue and green.
Aurora's dawn, arriviste, chroma rich!

The night's fractured like cymbal's heinous pitch
Holy lands dare dream of peace so serene,
Whilst night sky pearls resplendently bewitch!

Joy and love shape quilts with hopeful stitches.
Yet, baby angels are tossed midst styrene,
Still, Aurora's dawn, arriviste, chroma rich!
Whilst night sky pearls resplendently bewitch!

Jan L. Hetherly
Mt. Vernon, TX

So interesting . . . using flowery words to describe such vile acts of humanity. But whatever it takes to get the attention of people with hearts for understanding and love. Do unto others as you would have them do unto you! Let there be love!

Oops!

The simple things they ask of me
I cannot seemed to do!
Washed the dishes,
broke but two.
Took care of the children,
Caught the flu.
Swept the floor,
Spilt the glue.
Made the bed...OOPS!
Master screamed, "who are you?"
Bathed the dog,
Turned him blue?!?
Cooked the meal,
Burnt the goo.
A job at the glassworks,
where everything is new!

Holly Melia
Monson, ME

Serving My Lord

Whatsoever we do Lord
We'll turn to you Lord

Whatsoever we see Lord
We'll search your word Lord

Whatsoever we hear Lord
We'll hear your voice Lord

Whatsoever we say
Whatsoever we do
We'll do for you Lord

Yes, whatsoever we say
Whatsoever we do
We'll be sure to honor You Lord

Doris Cox
Tunnel Hill, GA

Thanks for my Sunday school teacher Darlene Beardon's words of encouragement.

Here Comes Summer

Summer has arrived ready or not, right on schedule
Heat and pop-up storms, maybe a rainbow
I've learned nothing can replace Gods' rain for plants,
especially those pesky weeds to thrive
Blue Jays squawking to remind me for peanuts
Squirrels sitting tall munching on left overs
Baby birds fluttering their wings, learn to fly
Chicken BBQ's, pool parties, family reunions
Sitting in traffic for a day at the beach
Produce stands display home grown goodies
Canning pickles, freezing corn, tomato sauce
Bike riding, kayaking, boats on the river, picnics
The never ending hum of a lawn mower
Kittens play, blooming flowers, bushes and trees
Fields of sunflowers, try to touch the clouds
Butterflies, humming birds, locusts chanting
Bees are busy flower to flower collecting nectar
Flies, ants and mosquitoes annoy me
I question Gods' reasoning for their existence
Lightning bugs light up the night, blink, blink
Out and about finding yard sales, treasures to find
Concerts in the park, movies after dark
Campfires, toasting marshmallows, s'mores
Sit in the sun, let Summer hug you with warmth
Cherish the memories, reflect on the adventures
Too soon you will say, "Where has summer gone."

Anita Rogers
Royersford, PA

Sitting on the porch, seeing and watching all summer has to offer unfold around me. Nature is truly amazing, ever-changing day to day.

The Babies Cry

Babies and children cry looking through the links
Loops and chains of a barrier never ending
Hidden from sight by a monster disguised as a man
Repeat of a history damned but not forgotten
Children torn from their mother's arms
Their parents sent to their own hell
Babies left to cry and scream for their mothers
Fathers helpless to protect, cry in their own torment
The babies cry, no arms to hold them
No mothers to calm them to dreams so sweet
The monster sits in the white house, a shamble, a mess
Not knowing what he is doing, in over his head
Over his head with power and might, his heart so tight
Heart cold devoid of feeling, closed to babies' cries
People hear and people speak, people cry out and shout
To be the voice of those too small, crying in the cages
No detail of parent and child, of who belongs to whom
Whisked away hidden from sight hiding what he has done
"Mama, Papa" the children cry with no answer
We feel the pain of the innocents
In prison-like camps not held nor comforted
Damage done to innocent souls we will not forget
There is love from the people, we'll fight and shout
We'll protest and cry out to the masses to hear us
Unite-Unite-Unite, this is not just their fight
We must fight for the babies and children at the border

Jill Taylor-Keck
San Rafael, CA

An Anniversary

A flurry of Monarch
And painted lady butterflies
Bursts from the blossoming mint,
As I tread the concrete walk
To the mailbox and maybe
An awaiting acceptance note
From a poetry publisher
On this October 22nd fall day,
You and dad were wed for 60 years
Before his heart just stopped,
And now eight years later
You still wear your wedding band.
As I write these lines to you,
In your heart you're still wed,
And I'll keep you both in my heart,
Until this poem turns to dust,
And the butterflies cease
To burst from the mint.

Richard Stepsay
Aurora, CO

Reflections of Roots

My heart
Is a warm rich brown
My skin
Unearthy white
My mind
Is red with anger
Burning in the midst
Of my black brothers plight!
For I had lived
Among such men
At such a ghastly time
History books
Would include the name
That of Janice Jane
May justice prevail…

Janice J. Dellolacono
Vernon, CT

Impulse

Had to roam.
Escaped at 16.
Found

    swift going
    slow going

    full streets
    empty streets

    loose money
    no money

    quick friends
    no friends

Just told by a street preacher,
Only 40 miles of rough road ahead
To reach Paradise.

Feet, don't fail me now!

Ron Matros
Mesilla, NM

Congratulations!

Congratulations!
I just heard the news—
Jackie is engaged
To Kathy's son.
Here are my views:

Jackie is a sweet girl,
And if she is engaged
To Kathy's son
She is also a lucky pearl
To tie the knot;
I kid you not.

So I wish you the best;
They will pass the test.
You know the rest.

Alfred Elkins
Bronx, NY

Pop

When I was small, you showed your love
In special ways that mean so much to me now.
I didn't know it then, but I was very lucky.

Your smiles of encouragement helped me
try, and learn, and to grow.
You seemed to know when I needed help and
advice . . . when I needed to be left alone
and when I needed someone to share the
tears that come with growing up.

I'm not sure how, but you did!

Thanks, Pop, for being there . . .
for understanding and for
being my friend as well as my Pop!

Scarlet Collins
Springtown, TX

Little Boy Gone

When you were young, you were my pride;
My love for you I couldn't hide.
So many things we used to do
I now must face without you.
We went to the doctor's office for you to be checked;
Little did I know then, my life would be wrecked.
He said that you were very sick, and nothing more.
I could feel the tears welling up in my eyes, as we walked out the door.
There were other doctors we went to see
But none of them would say what was most important to me.
As time went on, you became very ill;
I felt your pain, as I always will.
I held your hand, as the days passed away,
Praying to God for you that was all I could say.
Near the end when you looked up at me,
I almost wanted a merciful God to set you free.
You've gone now, as I watch the setting sun,
Part of my life will be missing without my only son.

Louis M. Graziaplena
Orlando, FL

Louis was born on September 16, 1942 at University Hospital on Greene Street in Baltimore, MD. He attended two different Catholic parochial schools—St. Brigid's and Our Lady of Pompei from which he graduated. After Catholic school he attended what was then Patterson Park High later to become Patterson High School, from which he graduated in February 1961. Eventually starting a career with the state of Maryland and retiring from the motor vehicle administration in June of 1994. After retiring he relocated to Orlando, FL where he presently resides. Louis was in the navy for four years and four months.

The Immortal Word

We are looking for God in all the wrong places,
because God is right behind our faces;
for God is the Immortal Word creating with an intensity
that projects supernal qualities thru mortal faculties.

By the principle of Omnipresence that manifests at birth
in all that God created and sustains on Earth
human life is experienced with the Word, as our choices define,
thru God's gift of mortal form in bodily designs.

Our function in the dimension of physical life will become clear
when we listen for guidance thru inner ear,
and allow the Creator abiding within
to lead us away from wanton temptations and the errors of sin.

When we acknowledge the spirituality of our transient being,
we'll behold a Divine Presence in all we are seeing.
We will know who is the I am of me
that makes God in our midst a reality.

We will understand the precepts for receiving and giving,
and the secrets of nature that make life worth living.
We will know we're all children in a family of one
with God as our heavenly Father and Source of life's creation.

Carol A. Sustarsic
Willowick, OH

"...and the Word was God," as cited in Scripture, glorifies the celestial energy uniting creation with God's breath of life. "And the life was the light of men." And whether we deny an incomprehensible supernal energy sustains life's creations, or accept it with a leap of faith, we experience the effects of its presence resonating throughout all mediums of communication we express our individualistic qualities in earthly forms. Ergo, we must be judicious with our words, as Scripture warns, lest societies bear the perpetual chaos and strife caused by unbridled tongues (John 1:1-4, 9; Ver. 4; Matt 12:36, 37; Jas 3).

My Guardian Angel

My mother was the most compassionate and warm-hearted woman I'd ever known. Strong, bright-spirited, and loving. My mom was the heart of our large family until a stroke left her depressed and short-tempered. Grumpiness was unlike my mom that her physician recommend a family member to step in on her psychiatric work-up. I, Karen, took on this job. I knew it would be hard, but it would be rewarding for my mother. So I took the job. We worked on her speech, her numbers; the doctor suggested that when I was there in her room alone to make her read newspaper articles and help her to sound out her words. Then count to ten and work up to one hundred. She got frustrated and through the paper down. I told her to scoot over in bed and we sat upright in her bed and I gave her the newspaper again and told her to "read." She looked at me and smiled. She read real good but her "I" and "E" sounds weren't quite right. Some words were quite funny. But, she was laughing and snuggling. I knew my mom was coming back to us. Mom's personality changed so much. It was like I found the mom I had always wanted . . . at ease, laughing, and being funny. When Mom was learning her numbers, for six she would say "sex," and when she got to sixty-six she would say sexty-sexty. I just about died laughing. One day the doctor told me he didn't know what I was doing but it was working. What did you do? he asked. I told him I just did what he told me to do. Before he left the room, I said, Doc, ask Mom to say sixty-six. He looked at me, then Mom and asked her. She looked at him with her mischievous eyes and said "Sexty-sexty." He looked at me, I smiled, and he turned with his hand high and walked out the door with a big smile. Mom and I laughed so loud; I'm sure everyone in the hospital heard us. When Mom got to go home, my hubby and I went to their home and played cards. Mom got up and went over to my dad and looked into his eyes. I said, Mom say sixty-six. She looked down and said "Sexty-sexty." My mom is gone now.

Karen S. Naber
York, NE

This prose poem is about my mother and her bout with a massive stroke. She lost feeling in a leg and arm and could hardly speak, but she was a fighter. The doctors requested the help of a family member and I told them I would do it. I went to the hospital every day and worked with her. It started working, and she was happy. I had never seen my mother so happy, laughing, and teasing. I'm so lucky I had this time with her. I miss her a lot.

Two Loving Seniors Sonnet

Two loving seniors are Sheila and I
Our love began twenty years ago
Our hearts mingled with each and every sigh
while we joined together very slow
Believing our health is worth more than wealth
She was disgusted how others would treat
Some busy-bodies deserve a big belt
This caused her to definitely overeat
Those folks should think and not overreact
Some remarks of others make us shutter
because they do not look for every fact
You see they do not care what they utter

She felt very hurt . . . both of us felt hurt
So does that define our love and our worth

Marvin D. Goldfarb
Sunnyside, NY

Lost and Lonely

Broke,
need a token to get home,
Tired of roaming around night after night,
Lost and lonely and bound in my mind,
wish I could find some kind of peace
and release of the pain in my brain
then I could refrain and not feel insane
from addiction to this pipe
that takes my pay and gets me high,
up, down, and bound all around
like a roller coaster.
Broke again no money it's not funny,
it's a vicious cycle day after day,
it's drugs I seek,
why am I so weak?
It's not cool, it's made me a fool,
thought you were my cure for all my pain
but what have I gained?
Thinking of the cost,
how did I get this lost?
There must be a better way,
here I lay in my grief with no relief,
ashamed of what my life has become.
I now want to fight to be free,
so I can be the man of God I was meant to be.

Margo Pennella
Jackson, NJ

I wrote this poem because I have a good friend who is battling an addiction and as I watch him and his life it breaks my heart. I try to help him but the addiction is more powerful, so he refuses help. He's such a good man, and I see so many others in this world with the same addiction and we are losing many to those drugs. My desire is to help as many people as I can get free from this deadly addiction.

I Can't Believe

The why of it all?
I can't believe

She so sweet
Outside to greet
The perfect girl

What torment stirred
Inside her painful heart
Could be to cause
Destruction of self

For loved ones now
To sorrow in grief
Around her coffin mourn
Missing her smiling voice

Outward so lively she lived
Pleasant her life
So thought to be
Concealed in beauty of expression
Her shield of pain
Disguising her mind of unrest
Until she has laid to out
To rest in peace

Daniel Valese
Nutley, NJ

Why Am I Here?

Where am I going, what is my name
Sometimes I feel I'm going insane.
Where am I going, what is my plan
Do I really know who I am?

Most of my family has passed away
But the future, I know, is planning my day.
Mom, Dad, sister, brother, husband, even a child.
I wonder, sometimes, why I'm still here for awhile.

I have two middle-aged children who love me true
And they never stop saying, "We'll take care of you."
But I want independence, I've got more living to do,
Can't you wait till you call me and I answer "who?"

Well, that day's approaching, to my dismay;
I have grown quite old, not much more I can say.
So, now what is my purpose in life at this age?
I'll tell you what I think—I'm a much needed sage!

Lois A. Goldstein
Lewes, DE

In a Moment

In a moment of my life
my life changed to you.

In a moment of praise
my voice lifted to you.

In a moment of my love
my heart accepted you.

In a moment of my adoration
my spirit connected to you.

In a moment of confidence
my heart obeyed you.

In a moment of worry
my problems were given to you.

In a moment of my life
my purpose changed to you.

In a moment of my silence
my worship was given to you.

In a moment of your sunset
my thanks were given to you.

In a moment, just a moment,
I recognized you.

Bonnie F. Tucker
Clarksburg, WV

Back into Infinity

In the uncertainty of chaos, we wear our smiles wide, wide,
In the miles as we travel with the gnawing
Jaws of Eternity nipping at our heels.
Conspiring with gravity— time burns through the energy that you are;
There is no dearth to the ineffable force that pursues you.
The earth with its soft, supple, soil is fertile and laden with vital rot
To help you ease your way back into infinity.
There is divinity in dirt.
The scent of the earth—the beauteous decay in your nostrils beckons
Gravity in concert with entropy patiently pulling you back into the soil
Blending you back into infinity.

Toni Jo Orban
Woodside, CA

Toni Orban is an English literature major at Notre Dame de Namur University. She has previous journalistic experience writing for the San Matean. She works as a personal trainer and massage therapist on the Central Coast of California. She is a free-lance health and fitness writer with past contributions to Planet Muscle *and* Hard Fitness Magazine. *She has several poems published in* The Bohemian. *She is looking to expand her writing to include her true passion poetry and fiction. She lives in Paso Robles, CA, with her two French bulldogs.*

Pulmonary Paradise

People pleasure pooped
Poppin' pills ploppin' popeyed
Patience proudly peppers pain
Pension planted plans
Peas pods panic
Posture poor panorama
Peelin' packin' pickin'
Pre-ordained priest password pizza
Pigeons prayin'
Petroleum prices payin'
Pulmonary paradise
Passing perfect passion
Pound per pound
Playin' poker pinup posters
Pacemakers penpal parties
Photogenic police
Photo finish please

Roy A. Smith
West Columbia, SC

Sap on My Shirt

I leaned upon a tree.
Its sap it shared with me.

I tried to brush it off.
The tree began to scoff.

On your shirt I left my imprint
A memory of your forest stint.

"A Kleenex will not work,"
Said the tree with a smirk.

With fingers I shall scrape quick.
Now they too are covered and stick.

Nothing left to do, oh Great Tree.
But take a part of you home with me.

Donna Walsh
Aurora, CO

Somewhere in Time for "Me"

This word has been sent from somewhere
In time a gift from (God) all mine. People I
can write poetry at the drop of a dime. So
I write this with no regrets about the most
handsome, kind, loveable, smartest man that
I have ever met. With wisdom like no other
so lets talk about him some more a little
bit further. A perfect gentleman he is human
and divine (not a man) so that please do
understand. He came into my life when I
needed him the most. In the person of the
(Holy Ghost). Always so very neat in the one
of a kind suit so sweet. When he came
after me I was bound and not so free. So
you see that was somewhere in time for
(him in my life with me). He came inside
of me to stay. And we will never separate
no how no way. So please hear me I do
pray. It is already done and the battle
has already been won. The time is growing
nigh for (God) to come back no lie.
And because my time is getting late I am
going to say to you (goodbye) and go
vacate.

Earline Hagwood
Columbus, OH

I live in Columbus, OH. I write poetry because it gives me joy and pleasure to write from my spirit what God has given to me. What a special precious gift that has been given to me by God; I give Him the honor and all the glory. I want to say, thank you, Lord Jesus, for all that you have done for me. Lord with all due respect, Earline love's and adores you now and forever.

Our Eyes

I do believe that our eyes are truly the window to our soul.
Some things that happen cannot always be explained.
Sometimes I believe that people can reach out to us after
leaving this world through people here on Earth.
I met a handsome young man one day while I was working.
When I looked into his eyes I felt this feeling in my heart
like my son was looking back at me; it took my breath away.
I explained this to this young man and to my surprise
he seemed like he knew what I meant. He was so compassionate
and understanding as I gently touched his cheek.
He asked me if he could hug me and I said, of course,
and there was an instant connection. I met his brother
not long after this and there was that same connection.
These two young men touched my life in a way I can't explain.
They were so gentle and caring just like my son I lost.
They had that same big heart like him and his beautiful
black eyes. A mother has a special bond with her children
that can't be broken even in death.
It was like these two were sent to me as a gift from my son
to say "Hi, Mom, I'm here with you." I will be forever grateful
for these two young men coming into my life and their
genuine kindness and compassion to someone they
didn't even know. They will always have a special place in my heart.
So the next time you have a chance to look into someone's
eyes, look very closely—you might be surprised at what you see!

Margaret Beach
Mechanicsville, MD

Thank You, Hero

Dear Veteran: Thank you, Pop-Pop
for protecting our country.
You are the best

Braden Olsen

The Line Between Night and Morning

The tip of my pen
Writes down my feelings
Just like I ask it to
My fingers
Type out the words
Expecting relief
From being honest
I sit in the dark
Feeling everything
Hoping one day
Someone cares enough
To read them
And understand
Hoping one day
Someone will sit with me in the dark
And help me feel new things

Angela Carlton
Pampa, TX

USAF Chad Marion Dingus, My Beloved Brother

At two, you were running and laughing here and there.
It did not suit your speed to remain seated in a chair.
Christmas presented you with a chance to box with me
Using your new boxing gloves found under the tree.
You gave me a punch that I couldn't possibly foresee
And knocked every bit of needed breath right out of me.
On your very first day of first grade you were found
To be wrestling a favorite cousin on the playground.
You tried to beat up the person who broke up your joy.
In your mind he was just another young high school boy.
Like you, this happened to be his first day, so uncool,
Of being the new principal of our elementary school.
As your big sister, a student in grade four,
I felt like an umpire when called to your door.
Shaking my pointing finger, I gave you the first degree,
Describing how angry and furious Mother would be.
"But I didn't know he was the principal," you cried.
This was a lesson long remembered with lost pride.
You graduated from Martin KY High School, making way
To join the United States Air Force for a future four-year stay.
Twice in May I dreamed of your drowning in a lake,
And wading into it, I intended your rescue to make.
Gathered in my arms, your image had a baby's look
And transformed into a ball of fire that Heaven took.
June 15, 1964, the US Air Force in Lake Folsom found you
Who died in Sacramento, CA, died June 13, 1964, age twenty-two.

Dollie Dingus
Danville, IL

As the oldest of ten children, I always tried to protect my brothers and sisters. Chad was very strong as a youngster and Mother took a picture of him at nine months old running from home. He was a delightful brother. I insisted on taking him with us when our brother Walter and I walked a mile to sell the grit paper. I loved all of my siblings and wouldn't take a million dollars for any of them. Four are deceased. Three, including myself, have had triple by-pass surgery. Thanks to God and modern technology, we are surviving.

The Stone

"Distance makes the heart grow fonder";
that's what they said as they tried to rip you from my embrace.
Each one who stepped forward thought only of you,
their eyes bearing down on you hungrily.
It became a personal challenge, who would be powerful enough
to tear you away from me?
And who can blame them? Your strength has lingered on tongues for
generations and you shine with a radiance that ancient alchemists
spent millennia failing to forge.
And, I, a mere grain of dust fortunate enough to exist on the same earth.
I had only tasted happiness when you were plunged into my life
to fill the hollow parts of me that the world had weathered away.
Each one who dared to lay his hands on you didn't think of me,
of the hole they would leave.
Their faces mirrored my surprise that we managed to hold on for so long,
that somehow an unlikely pair had found harmony.
On a fateful day, one stranger cast you aside.
On a fateful day, a new stranger claimed you.
I remember the gleam in his eye as he drew you away from me
and you offered no protest, no backwards glance, because he was the one.
Through the years I have heard the tale of Romeo and Juliet repeated,
a story that has made romance and death synonymous.
My life began and ended with your arrival and departure, yet I remain
for you are the sword, and I am but the stone.

Sawyer Emily Scott
Denton, MD

I wrote this poem in my final year of undergraduate studies, at a time when I was trying to discern if I should reignite my childhood dreams of being a writer. While I never found a clear-cut answer, I did find this poem. I wanted it to be a testimony from an ancient perspective that is never considered, and yet one that describes a situation that resounds with tones of modern relationships to this day. I hoped to give the stone a voice through this short poem, and I like that it came out very realistic instead of overly fantastical. Enjoy!

Song of Salvation

God bless our USA today
Bless wicked-world from day to day
Our leaders failed to bring world-peace
'tis why terrorism must cease
Heavenly Father keep world from harm
while living in town or on farm
when Christ comes back to earth
He will fill pure hearts w/mirth
If his will we obeyed while alive
Eternal H-e-l-l we will survive

Ollie V. Zoller
Amarillo, TX

I wrote this poem to encourage God's children to continue walking in Jesus' footprints every day. To y'all still sinning in a wicked world, don't wait! Do be reborn today! I married William Eugene Zoller, a WWII/Korean Conflict veteran. Bill was a graduate accountant. Me? A homemaker. When I lost Bill at age sixty-two on July 3, 1989 I almost lost my mind. But after writing poems and short articles I relaxed from my anxiety. I whole-heartedly thank y'all for printing them.

Hello Kitty

Casey "Hello Kitty" brought
everyone much love.
I still feel the connection,
Only now from above.

She's now with her loved ones
in the by-and-by.
Having much fun in her
mansion in the sky.

Casey loved "Hello Kitty,"
just like me.
Her and I were caring friends
and we still be.

Our love for "Kitty"
was the same.
In fact, Casey liked being
called "Kitty's" name.

For Casey, I gladly
wrote this ditty.
All in Heaven are
saying "Hello Kitty".

Sandra Begeer
Santa Rosa, CA

I wrote this poem in honor and loving memory of Acacia "Casey" Chastain. We all miss her a lot. Love you, Casey!

Happy Holidays

The wind is blowing
There's a chill in the air
The snow starts to fall
Christmas is almost here
The tree is up, decorations, too
Glowing red, green and blue
Rudolph's nose is shining
Frosty is around to see
Families get together
Whether they live far or near
To say "Happy Holidays" and
to spread good cheer

Candace M. Slisz
New Britain, CT

Birth of the Star Queen

Birth of The Star Queen, Origin of Shield-Maiden
Why speak in such terms when her glory is Eternal
The King of All knew her before worlds began
And I, I know her glory
She sits serene on her throne, it's pillars, my hearts creation
Upon Calabi–Yau spheres rest her feet
In gleaming universe, no multi-verse she's seen
Suns are birthed, my love complete
I see my Queen, The Star Queen...

Charles Worthy
Gig Harbor, WA

Living in Gig Harbor WA, I enjoy writing poetry on a wide range of topics, love, life and my struggles. One of my prime inspirations is my wife who inspires much of my poetry. All the best, Chuck Worthy

A Wonderful Mother

Beauty within, you are so true
My words can't even describe
A mother like you
You showed me happiness
Raised me right, not wrong
You showed me this world
I'm right where I belong
I was raised to respect, treat others with kind
Be warm and gentle, never leave anyone behind
You treated me well, your heart having so much love
I know now you were sent to me
From the heavens above
'Cause an angel is with me in all I do
Now I am starting to believe that angel is you
So to my angel
Who watches over me day and night
Thank you for always walking with me
Teaching me how to live right
I will love you forever and always to be
Know I respect you, you mean the world to me
A wonderful mother, I have no doubt
And all those special cherished moments
Is what life is all about

Amy Allen Hale
Hohenwald, TN

I never realized just what my mother gave up and sacrificed for me growing up and throughout my years. She always went out of her way putting me and my family first before her own needs and I wanted to let her know just how much I respected her and appreciated her for what she did for me and this is what gave me the inspiration for "A Wonderful Mother."

A Great Loss

I see you standing
outside in the rain
your heart keeps pounding
from the pain
that remains
Life is a gift
is so often your told
but sometimes we
feel like life can't unfold
Just turn to the sky
and you'll find some hope
When someone you love
is in Heaven you know
Know that there
With you
threw all that is bad
there standing beside you
in the pouring rain

Corena M. Elmer
Elk River, MN

Linda is a good friend of mine from Milaca, MN. She recently lost her amazing son who had two children. My heart just bleeds for her because there is no greater pain in the world than grief, especially when it's due to the loss of a child. So I want to dedicate this poem to her and her husband. My prayers are always with them, and I hope God will guide them and help them heal. To comfort them, I know in my heart their loving son is in Heaven.

On This Planet

I'm still alive for a reason
In our galaxy I still didn't see
All the girls in our world who are teasing
And sometimes these girls flirt with me
Guess I can't marry on this planet
Put enough skills in my resume
Filled it up a lot when I ran it
But not enough rhymes from me did I say
Growing food for all on this season
To give fruits and vegetables from me
Everyone to stay younger and have fun
In this universe they'll stay here more healthy
Didn't find nice Mars girls or Mercury
Through my long space mind telescope
Venus ladies were the shooting stars
And Jupiter's women used so much soap
Planet Nine ones are closer to Pluto
Gals spin the wheel when you're visiting Saturn
Don't forget Neptune or from Uranus
Far away from the sun you won't burn
Single astronaut men in their rocket
Use the sun on their skin just to tan it
Keep ideas to travel in their pocket
Here on Earth for a date gotta plan it
One mistake is their heart when they lock it
We have so much to fix on this planet

Juan R. Nogales
Calexico, CA

Hello, today March 30, 2020, thousands of people in the world have died from Corona virus. Many are in lines trying to receive their unemployment benefits. People are purchasing large amounts to stay away from everyone. In my front yard I have fifty trees and three hundred plants. In May, being a Catholic scientist, I'll give away my fruits and vegetables to everyone for free. I haven't been sick for forty-seven years so I know I'll make many people healthier and live longer. I'll keep writing songs to try to get famous and I will always love my daughter Natasha Arambula forever.

It Only Takes a Moment

It only takes a moment
To do a thoughtful thing.
Just think of all the happiness
Our thoughtful acts might bring.
Why, it only takes a moment
To pick up the telephone
And say "Hello" to someone
Who is sitting home alone.
It will only take a moment
To extend a helping hand
Or give someone assurance
That we really understand.
Yet each moment is God given
In our acts of kindness
Because it only takes a moment.

Alma M. Gaines
New Rochelle, NY

Guide me in Your truth and teach me, for You are God my Savior and my hope is in You all day long. Psalms 25:5

Court of Public Opinion I

I never knew her name
But I feel her pain
I know from whence it came
The world looked on in disdain
Tried and convicted she passed
Sentence on herself tears fell like confetti
Condemned and judged already
By the court of public opinion
They all looked the other way
No one ever saw her tears
Although they always had a lot to say
Never cared about her fears
There seemed to be
A concerted effort of
Folks who wouldn't see
And couldn't show love
She had her dog
Who was her friend
Even through the fog
Right to the end
Her dog was there
Every minute every day
And always did care
Trying to love the pain away
While they are at peace
I find myself wondering
How we turn a blind eye with such ease
Allowing ourselves to exhibit such orgulous behavior

Latitia Mariner
Happy, TX

So many people suffer alone with mental illness. What happened to compassion, Christian values, and love your neighbor? Love those who can't love themselves. Ink memory of a lost soul who wandered alone in her sorrow. Who will God judge?

The One Thing Needful

Start each day with thoughtful prayer
End each day like you began
And through the day, stop and pause
Be thankful, you are in God's hand

Don't get distracted, worried
Forgetful or hurried
Take time out, get in touch
With your Saviour, He loves you much

Many things want our attention
Smart TV's, cars, computers, new inventions
Websites, games, apps and smart phones
Just a few to mention

With every purchase, Warning! Use wisely
When using, my warning recall
To put these gadgets first in your life
They may not be smart after all

If you want to be smart
Put God first in your heart
With priorities straight, be heedful
You'll find out, Jesus, He is the one thing needful

Linda J. Knudsen
N. Mankato, MN

And Jesus answered and said unto her, Martha, Martha, thou art worried and troubled about many things. But one thing is needful: and Mary hath chosen that good part, which shall not be taken away from her. (Luke 10:41, 42)

The Light Behind My Eyes

The light behind my eyes
Shines in shades of blue
Reflecting island symbols
Within myriad hues

The light behind my eyes
Shines when my lids are closed
In my overcast room
As I begin to doze

The light behind my eyes
Now fading to pale blue
Reminiscent paisley
Of pineapple and palm

The light behind my eyes
May it not fade away
As sight dims more each day
I will watch the shadows play

In the light behind my eyes

Sharon W. King-Jeffers
Albuquerque, NM

We moved to Hawaii several years ago after four decades of vacations in paradise. I wrote this poem while recovering from surgery in the hospital for an extended period of time. This strange phenomena of blue light and identifiable objects when I closed my eyes at night was strange but beautiful. I can still see, but my vision was clouded by cataracts at that time.

The Adopted Child

Once upon a time
there was a little black pauper girl with 4 siblings
in a box.
All were very scared but the little baby girl was trembling horribly.
A lady came to see them,
The little pauper pensively contemplated,
"This lady came to see us and started playing with all of us,
she seems to be kind-hearted, but
I don't want to leave my siblings.
She seemed interested in me, but left."
A bell rang,
"the young girl came to pick me up
to take me to the lady.
I was shaking, I was taken in a box with wheels to another place,
I could feel my ears coming down.
Minutes later, wow a palace.
From then on, I became a princess.
My story is a Disney story—
from pauper to princess."
"I still suffer from separation anxiety disorder,
that's what my soul mate says,
going in a car gets me very nervous,
and watching a truck drive by us makes me shiver.

Daphne Martinez
San Juan, PR

Thanksgiving and Peace and Love

One cannot be thankful and not have peace!
I choose joy. No sorrow. I choose peace!
No hatred. I choose harmony. No chaos.
One cannot say there is no love.
Love surrounds me until my cup is overflowing.
One cannot tell me there is no love. People
crave it more than candy in the stores.
People tell me there is no God. God's word,
the Bible, tells us He is alive and well, living in us who believe.
God lives in our hearts, our minds, our souls.
He is always with us to the end of time as we know it.
In olden days just like today many fought wars
over greed, money, and fame for selfishness sake
or pure hate's sake.
Brothers fighting brothers, sisters fighting sisters,
dads fighting sons, moms fighting daughters.
Come on, people, we are better than this!
Without love we are absolutely nothing.
Light those candles, give love another try.
We the people of the world, for our children
and their children demand the world and the
leaders to give peace and love another try!

Rhonda R. Carden
Moultrie, GA

Many people are praying for the USA and fellow Americans all across our country. Politicians, many find disgusting, need to find a new job. They want respect but they need to learn how to give respect to we the people. Many Americans love everyone with no hate towards anyone. The United States needs to see we all deserve love and respect and to not be fighting with our family, neighbors, and friends. We voted them into office but they forget we can vote them out, too! America is about love, forgiveness, new beginnings, not hating or fighting one another, but helping and giving hugs and having laughter in us, not tears.

Risen After the Storm

I dragged my feet through the dirt and muddy water
Where a lone rag doll floats on
As the sun rises with my head held high I journey on
The wishes for dry land are hopeful.

The pieces make sense past this devastation
As the rush of crashed emotions overcomes me
I know in these moments of my life hardships will pass.

I picked up my soiled pictures in the aftermath
And pray with a wholeness that helps get me through.

Partial to the wisdom of another day
Full of this miracle my breath is still in my lungs
Food is provided even though every store is hollow
As a temple of abundance yet to be given.

Making use of these moments virtue
To save a passer-by and pick them up
Out of the rushing waters with so much left inside.

I am moving my ankles through broken debris
Living in faith for a chance to see my son once more
Wherever the river takes him I will go.

Mariah DeLorenzo
Homeland, CA

Poetry is a part of who I am, my passion. Through my emotions, love of nature, music, and gratitude for my life experiences, I feel inspired and deeply compelled to write. What inspired me to write my poem, "Risen After the Storm," was remembering the images, magnitude, and devastation of what people went through during the 2017 hurricanes Harvey (Texas) and Irma (Florida). I observed how people came together to overcome obstacles and turmoil of the divide, regardless of any discrimination. There is higher power within us to feel love, deep compassion, and connection as one for our survival.

Magical Eyes

My first love…
Captured my heart
With his magical eyes
They pierced into my soul
And whispered to me
Of dreams and desire.
I was hypnotized
By his eyes…

But he went away
And seasons bow to no one
I searched for magical eyes
Throughout the years
In other places
And other faces
Never found again

But the morning star of destiny
Heard the empty echo
Of my heart
And the beautiful distant eyes
Returned to me
Memories, dreams and desires
Were still masked there
Now, when he says "I love you"
I see it in those magical eyes
Still hypnotized…

Donna J. Shaver
Laurens, NY

I dedicate this poem to John D. Robinson, Phoenix Mills, Cooperstown, NY. Our story began long ago as teenagers in love. After two-and-a-half years we parted and went on to live very different lives. We only occasionally ran into each other throughout the many years. But a bond of our friendship always remained as we wished each other well. Now we have reached eighty plus years and our eyes have found one another again to share and finish our love story together.

Listen to the Trees

The wind begins, like a conductor
with his medley of sounds.
The trees respond echoing their
variety of different recourse,
trying to remain on key before
the wind pauses to say no more.
Then by some strange manner
Mother Nature intervenes and by and
by at her calling, the leaves start falling.
As if it's a game of follow the leader,
they drop to their destiny.
Henceforth the sounds are over
and the ground is covered by the rapture
of the trees.

Daniel P. Kraft
Warrenton, VA

As a veteran with a disability, I thank God every day that my daughter is the light of my life. Without her life would be nothing. I remember the oath I took in the army—my God, my country, and then me. I never forgot it. I once sat in a field of clover and in one and a half hours I found eighty-four four-leaf clovers. Tell me I'm lucky.

Hope

Life is you when air
flows to my heart
Teach me to walk a loving
path that shines with love
The light of your path
shows the love
How your precious love
withstands the streams
that come my way
Love comes from you
beyond the space
which grows with time

PJ Olivas
Needville, TX

Issues

Once more, another
year is upon us.
It's emerging from a
deep and chilling sleep.
This is extremely unique.
There are many reasons
for each season.
Climatic change is affecting
everybody and everything.
Daily, we have major happenings.
Dramatic debates dwell in this election.
Love and respect for each other
are totally humane actions.
These humane actions are near and dear.
These humane actions can last
for many, many years.

Pauline Eurica Blagrove
San Antonio, TX

The Walk

If walks could talk, they'd say:
As your gait carries your weight from the left to the right
and as you glide into your stride every step is forward—
always without fail.
All the feet must now seek is its trail.
With every step taken, we awaken a fiber that feeds the brain.
Every breath then wires and inspires thoughts of our own...
deep and real . . . .
They reveal the very best of ourselves.
Go take a walk and have that talk . . . that beckons

Hannie J. Voyles
Whitefish, MT

Heart to Heart

From my heart to your heart I am sending you my love
To you on the wings of a snow white dove!
From my heart to your heart I am sending you my love!
Not for just a day but for always and forever I am sending you my love!
Open up your heart and receive this love divine
For I love you truly and hope that you will be mine!
I pray that I am the love that you have waited for
So we can be together for now and for always and forevermore!

Richard P. Hemmen
Dixon, IL

I dedicate this poem to my wife Sharon, the love of my life. She has a heart of gold and I'm lucky to have her in my life.

Christmas Brings Joy, Tears, and Terror

Christmas in America brings thoughts of joy, gifts,
Holiday cards, bright lights on evergreen trees,
Festive decorations, red ribbons, and plenty to eat.
Visions of sweet treats, turkey, dressing, and bowls of
Grandmother's fruit salad with whipped cream can
Make our expectations more than supreme.
 All of these annual rites are brought about by the
Christians celebrating the birth of Jesus, the Christ
Child, God's gift to the world.
 While America's christians gather in joy, Christmas
In the anti-Christ nations of China, North Korea, and
Sudan prepare for tears and terror from church raids
By police, arrests, interrogations, public beatings,
And even death as they gather to worship God and
Celebrate the birth of the Messiah, Jesus.
 You see, the anti-Christ police know christians plan
Special events at this time of the year so they plan
Raids on churches where children are arrested, young
Girls are disrobed and abused, pastors are beaten
Unconscious and many die. Sudan's christians face all
The same horrors as well as genocide and annihilation.
 Let us remember to pray for these persecuted
Christians in anti-Christ lands as we light our own
Candles in celebration this Christmas.

Mable M. Guiney
Ft. Walton Beach, FL

I am a former coal miner's daughter who lived in Mingo County's #24 Coal Camp in West Virginia while in elementary school. My family migrated to Cleveland, OH when the mines closed and my dad found a job at General Motors. After high school graduation I began working for the Cleveland Trust Bank in downtown Cleveland. I saved money for college tuition and then entered Evangel University in Springfield, MO. I graduated with a BS in elementary education and began teaching students in Missouri, Kansas, and Utah. Later I joined the United States Army Reserves and became sergeant first class.

The Garden Gate of Dreams

A rosy glow on cheeks, blushed by reflection
Her soft privy thoughts cause sanguine complexion
Every posy rose in the garden knows why
The deep colors of his love tend to make her cry
She has missed his lingering kiss of late
Waking to chagrined change from twist of fate
Nature bows, giving her reverent passage
An aroma of wooing words' sweet adage
She walks down lush, laden aisles of orchid grace
Each perfumed petal waves hope in interlace
Keeping her captive in their merry musing
A delightful landscape of vibrant fusing
Down each row, she starts to show faith's favor
Lost in frosted thoughts of love's sweet savor
She imagines him crossing the floral field
As if he feels her heart's radiant appeal
It's true! In full flowering view, he'll find her
To embrace her fantasies with kind reminder
He lingers by the garden gate of dreams
To hold her as his own, for love to redeem

Cherie Leigh Sumner
Denver, NC

Attempt

I know one day I'll take that step
I can forgive but I can't forget
The tears are dry but I've still wept
The mess exists even though I swept
I've cried myself to sleep in every place I've slept
My cuts are healed but the scars are kept
The secrets are out, done, and gone but still you crept
My surface is beautiful although my mind is unkempt
I am free from all charges, still lacking exempt
I know one day I'll take that step
And kill myself, not just attempt.

Alexandra Rose Alcaraz
Norco, CA

Hi I'm Alexandra and I'm twenty years old. I've been writing poetry since the fifth grade, and everything I write stems from my life or my feelings. Poetry has always been a big part of my life and the easiest way for me to express myself. I hope you guys like what you read and I hope I can make you feel something.

Apsaalooke's Invisible Warrior

Upon a red and white pinto he proudly sits,
Eyes fixed upon his brothers, the Apsaalooke,
And their mortal enemies the Cheyenne, Sioux, and Arapaho.
He remains on the sidelines unseen by the Crow.
The Crows, also known as the Apsaalooke, are out-numbered,
Which was often the case, but their courage was well-known.
Their enemies surrounded them with lust for destruction.
But a champion is within their midst with another deduction.
This mighty warrior unseen by the Crow but well-known by the enemy
Waited for the challenge from the enemy before he attacked.
With a blood-curdling war whoop he began his retaliation.
He moved swiftly slaying the enemy to save the Crow nation.
The enemy lay upon the ground they once coveted as their home
While many more of them fled with fear in their hearts.
The Crows knew not of their champion, but the enemy surely did.
Who was this great warrior unknown to the Crow who did rid?
These enemies who wished to steal that which belonged to the Crow
Desired the Crow's land, women, children, and property.
But a greater power protected the Crow from a deadly fate,
Sending a champion to protect the Crow before it was too late.
Only through the traditions of other native nations did the Crows
Learn of this mighty warrior who sat upon a red and white pinto.
A great warrior who has no name yet is a hero among the Crow.
Great is his legacy, great is his gift, a great man to know.

Alice Marie Young-Lionshows
Lodge Grass, MT

My name is Alice Marie Young-Lion Shows. I am an enrolled member of the Crow Nation, which is located in southeastern Montana surrounded by the beautiful Big Horn Mountains. I have resided on the Crow Indian Reservation, also known as the Apsaalooke Nation, for much of the seventy-two years of my life. At the present time I am a retired school teacher but in my retirement I have chosen to aid defendants in the Crow Tribal Court System in the areas of juvenile, civil, and criminal law. But the time I spend writing poetry is the most rewarding.

Worship Him Who Made Heaven

I heard a voice from heaven,
Saying worship Him who made heaven.
Even in very difficult times,
You must keep all God's commandments.
Then three angels appeared and surrounded my bedside,
Helping to fulfill God's promise as a witness of saving me.
Prayers of family, friends, and Bible uplifting scriptures
Gently reassured me of God's greatest comfort.
My heartache of life struggles is over!
I passed away as a believer in the Lord,
Resting from my labors of work.
The angels swiftly carried my spirit up,
God's stairway to heaven.
Upon my arrival seven angels stood on
Each side of the pearly gates,
Blowing their trumpets in the air as my
Spirit made entrance inside heaven.
Now I have wings like a dove!
I will continue to fly watching over all my loved ones,
And be at holy rest.

Vonda Howard
Milwaukee, WI

My name is Vonda Elizabeth Howard, I live in Milwaukee, WI. I studied business and management at Concordia University of Wisconsin. Upon writing this poem, I always mind travel down memory lane of my family and friends who passed away. This time I thought about myself passing away in this poem and how eternal life would be transitioning to the other side.

Vitality

Cultivate and maintain a meaningful and purposeful existence
    with a strong, compelling affection, desire, enthusiasm, and excitement
    for learning and experience.
Embrace nature with the senses and see, hear, taste, smell, and touch
    the world with eagerness, stimulation, and certitude.
Elicit exuberance and fervor of mental and physical energy and strength
    toward life goals pursued.

Nurture feelings of curiosity and inquisitiveness with a thirst for
    knowledge amidst a yearning for wisdom in a search impledge.
Query cognitively and want to know about the world around
    by allowing speculations, mediations, and reflections to abound.

Have an appreciation, admiration, and adoration for the wonders, riddles,
    and mysteries life has to offer, while being filled with vim, vigor, and
    vitality, seeking and assessing every answer.
Be zealous and carried away with joy, delight, and pleasure; feel the
    overpowering rapture and ecstacy these states can assure.

Become alive, aroused, and energized *in* life, not merely an inanimate,
    passive, inactive member *of* it by expressing spontaneity, creativity,
    originality, inventiveness, explorativeness, and wit.
The purpose of life is living, not merely existing, whereby it is astonishing,
    awakening, bewildering, challenging, encouraging, marvelling,
    questioning, pleasuring, saddening, and shimmering!

Peter O. Peretti
Chicago, IL

To My Love

Chubby little angel, there
In your crib of white and blue,
Smiling sweetly up at me,
Little cherub, I love you!

Now your thumb is in your mouth;
There's a twinkle in your eye
That outshines the stars above
In the blue and sparkling sky.

Though you squall at dinnertime,
Wrinkling up your little face,
You can win my heart again
With your baby charms and grace.

For you my love will ne'er grow cold,
Though all else may prove untrue.
You are only three months old,
And my love will grow with you.

Ruth E. Brugler
Burghill, OH

The Peaceful Valley

When my eyes close in death
I pray to wake up in
Heaven's peaceful valley!

Where the Son of God
Will shine bright
In our heavenly home!

Peace and happiness
Will be forever and ever!
We'll never be lonely again!

No troubles or cares
To bring tears to our eyes
No more broken hearts
The pleasures I want are
To praise the Father
The Son, and the Holy Ghost for ever!

Maxine Harville
Bay Minette, AL

You're the Gift of Everything

Your beautiful qualities are too numerous to count.
Your brilliance shines brighter than the sun.
The wisdom you give is always laced with compassion.
You're the gift of everything.
People in your life be they family, friends or even strangers,
Know you as a true blessing in their lives.
And consider themselves very lucky.
You're the gift of everything.
Your gorgeous smile is the true pathway to great friendships.
Your sincerity to truly living always spring from the beautiful
Soul you carry with you.
You're the present we always need.
You're the gift of everything.

John Mark Tolbert
Savannah, GA

Thank you for the chance to speak from my soul. Bless my family for giving me courage and heart. This is dedicated to Gabrielle Arden Padley—a whole lot of name for a whole lot of woman. She personifies grace, warmth, and style. Her intelligence and spirituality shine brighter than all the stars in Heaven. What she brings to the table of life is so simple. It's called pure joy. She's the kind of woman the classic movie lines were made for. Is she worth fighting for? No, she's worth dying for. As for me she's the gift of everything.

Tanzania

I've seen the plains and valleys of Africa
Sat beneath an old acacia tree
Braved the coastal waters off Zanzibar as the sun beat down on me
I walked the Serengeti and marveled at Killimanjaro's height
But my fondest memories will always be of those Tanzanian nights
As time stood still I was mesmerized by that painted sky and those stars shining down on me.
Beautiful lights, spirited lights as though it was a Christmas tree
The sky was aglow with countless stars bright and glimmering near and afar.
Flickering lights from distant worlds eons and eons away.
I still envision them as though it was yesterday

Ronald E. Honis Jr.
Teaneck, NJ

Am I Just a Memory?

Passionate kisses, time on the phone
   Now I am feeling all alone.
Dancing to music, smiles on our faces
   Now I am feeling too much space.
I am a singular being, please refer to me as such,
   Comparing me to others doesn't mean so much.
You used to say I was everything to you;
   Now I just feel like something on the sole of your shoe.
Who's more important, I think it's clear;
   You're always so distant when I am near.
So many things we used to be
   Are all just a memory.

Kathleen Rose Donnelly
Sidney, MT

Our Family

Always behaving and obedient,
people wondered: what's their secret?
Always requesting by Mom to "all get along,"
which was reinforced by Dad's strong arm.
We were ten and all worked together on the farm.
Our two brothers in the fields and in the barn,
the seven girls worked as they were able
in the gardens, fields, or setting the table.
On Sundays, after feeding the milking the cows,
went to church then the evenings were ours.
The brothers entertained us with music and guitar,
then sometimes took us for a ride in the car.
We grew up and picked a partner of our own
and started a family, making a new home.
Many years passed and our hair turned white.
God watched over us in our failing eye sight.
Some God has taken to Heaven;
I'm one of the three left—
I'm number seven.

Edith Owen
Raleigh, NC

Best Poets of 2019

The Path Seemed Long This Day

the path seemed long this day
I stopped to catch a breath
by the way side
and to ponder
still, a mere half the walk ahead
the tree I leaned up against
no hurry, stay for a time
I listened to the forest
for quite a long while
the air was fresh
spring's most colorful face smiled all around
at that spot by the way side
just a mere half the walk ahead
I drew another breath
the path seemed long this day

Thomas A. Taylor
Shelton, WA

Love Comes Softly

They say that love comes softly
Like a silent summer breeze
A slow inviting pleasure
A soft caress, a touch, a tease
It wraps you gently in its arms
Surrounding all your senses
Enticing, playful, subtle, warm
It captivates, and cleanses

They say that love comes softly
Like the slowly rising waves
From deep within the ocean
A cool refreshing spray
The whisper of the water
As it meets the shore and then
Slowly to retrace its path
As its journey starts again

They say that Love comes softly
Like unhurried springtime rain
Tantalizing, Tempting
As it quietly calls your name
And once you feel its splendor
You'll never be the same
For they say that love comes softly
As the spark becomes a flame

Lesa Costa
Redding, CA

After failed marriages and a suicide, I learned I can make it on my own.

I Am Tired

I am tired of being the broken one.
I am tired of being the one disappointed.
I am tired of being told not to burn bridges.
I am tired of being the one to hold it together.
For I was not the one playing with fire.
I was not the one who lit the match.
And I am tired of being the one to watch it burn
While the arsonist skips away.
I am tired.
So, I will no longer tolerate being disappointed.
I will no longer be ignored.
I will no longer bear the burden of the bridge.
I will no longer deal with the ashes.
For I have promised myself to wear my crown,
To own my kingdom.
To stand strong
To Have my own back
For they should have expected the spark
And know that the bridge would burn.
For I am done being that person.

Laurie Howland
Milford, OH

I am a writer, mother to an amazing eye-rolling teenager, wife and small business owner who spends every day putting weight to paper to better understand myself and the world around me. I am grateful for every moment that allows me to do this. I wrote this poem off of a journal writing I did after having a friend greatly disappoint me. As my husband tried to convince me to simply let it go, I realized that I am always the one letting it go. Not rocking the boat. And I am tired of being that person.

Going Home

Eternity begins with a whisper without the slightest sound
As our spirit leaves our body and becomes heaven bound
Going to be with Jesus near God's heavenly throne
A place to enjoy of untold beauty, this heaven our new home
A place prepared by Jesus when he ascended above
And filled it with his beauty and his never-ending love
A mansion he promised to each of his redeemed
Where they will live forever and his glory they will glean
Singing and dancing continually on those golden avenues
Giving us that blessed assurance that one day we will be singing and dancing too

Arvel E. O'Brien Jr.
Columbia, TN

This poem was written for a friend whose father had passed away. The night after he passed I was awakened at midnight with these words going through my mind. So I got up and wrote them down immediately. I have shared this poem with numerous people who have lost loved ones. I give God the glory for inspiring this poem and others.

Beautiful Love

The question that was asked
was simple and direct
by a dear old gentleman
who'd been put through the test.
What is more beautiful
than the young love?
The gentleman smiled his answer.
Old love from above.
Young love's about each other.
A special beauty is seen.
A beginning of new days.
All things especially keen.
Old love marks changes,
struggles holding two together,
empty nests, diseases spread wings,
A love of years not severed.
So the answer to the question
What's more beautiful
than the young love?
Like Jesus' love and caring,
It's old love guided from above.

Loraine Faschingbauer
Bloomer, WI

A Tribute to Anna

I never knew that you would just walk into my life
Was it just coincidence—who knew?
For when you walked into my ife
It was that perfect moment, a true moment,
Just when I needed someone!
Although at the time you didn't know it
Mom you had also needed me!
Was it just coincidence?
For you had been more than just a
Dog named Anna!
You had become my companion, my friend
As you also Mom, my companion, my friend.
For we went for long walks in the park:
I got to run in the sand on the beach.
Mom, you took me everywhere;
We had so much fun!
When I became sick you still took care of me!
Until I was no longer able
To hold onto life.
But, in time, you would let me go.
Thank you. So was it all just coincidence?

Dorothy Safko
Manchester, PA

Apocalypse

Apocalypse
Revelation's damnation
Old Eden was Adam's apocalypse
Analysis: prophetic destination
No freedom in Satan's desecration
Aslan the Great
The father of creation and salvation
Apocalypse hell is Satan's final destination
The lamb, dragon's fate
He who has an ear, listen to what the spirit
has to say to the church. Hear it.
He who has a voice, *gloria spiritui sancto*
He who has no choice, glory be to the Holy Spirit
First apocalypse is seven seals of creation. Horror!
Second apocalypse is seventh seal and the golden censor. Horror!
Third apocalypse is the beast rising from the sea. Horror!
Fourth apocalypse is the second beast rising from the earth. Horror!
Fifth apocalypse is seven angels with seven plagues. Horror!
Sixth apocalypse is the great prostitute and the beast. Horror!
Seventh apocalypse is fall of Babylon. Horror!
Revelation's damnation
Apocalypse.

Timothy A. Wik
Elkins Park, PA

Father with God in Heaven

Papa, nothing prepared me for losing you,
Even though I knew this day, would soon come true.
More than a father, you were also my dad,
The very best anyone has ever had.

In my heart I have saved our special place,
No one can fill or try to replace.
There is peace and comfort, now that you are out of harm,
Knowing you're in God's loving, outstretched arms.

I used to lean on you for everything,
To stand firm in an unstable world, full of scary things.
Your shoulders feel so far from me now,
But I will manage to lean somehow.

I hope I make you happy and proud,
As you cheer me on from Heaven's crowd.
It seems as though you are right beside me,
Slaying the dragons that can't be seen.

Show me what I need to discern,
There are so many lessons I still need to learn.
You taught me how to stand on my two feet,
Now watch over me, from Heaven's Mercy Seat.

So far away and yet so near,
I will move forward with little fear.
Because my daddy has gone on before,
I'll join him some day on Heaven's shores.

Aida Maria Guran
Surprise, AZ

I wrote this poem in memory of my dad who passed away to Heaven from this earth and I want my dad to know how much I love him, my stepdad, because we had a strong relationship and he loved me as much as he would were I from his own blood!

Climate Change

Climate change is real.
God ordained Noah to build an ark in which he and his
family took shelter, along with species of animals and birds.
Then God purified the earth with constant rain until it flooded.
When it subsided he made a covenant with Noah.
"Let there be seed time and harvest, cold and heat,
summer and winter, day and night shall not cease."
Man disobeyed God's commandments by establishing industrial
factories which developed greenhouse gas known as carbon
dioxide which created climate change that warms the global hemisphere.
The Antarctic continent covered with a sheet of ice is dissolving due
to climate change.
Also lofty mountains covered with snow are melting.
Mr. Santa Claus, Mrs. Claus, the elves, and reindeers have to find
a new home because the North Pole is thawing due to climate change.
Other sources attributed to climate change are the launching of
rockets into space, planes traversing in the sky releasing combustible
fumes into the atmosphere.
Volcanoes eject gases and arsenic sprays impregnating the atmosphere.
Ocean levels are intensifying. Elements are magnetizing.
Penguins at the North Pole struggle to survive due to climate change.
Fires, smoke, and cars' gaseous vapors contribute to climate change.
Insects and wildlife animals are becoming obscure.
Indeed it's an international problem.
Congress and other countries have to enact laws to generate new
technologies to halt global warming.

Wilbert Roberts
Port St Lucie, FL

Christmas of TD's

Initials perfect.
Christmas of TD's
Cool, hard, romantic
is super teen's magic and spaceship
Original future true dreams.

My coke is red
I am not blue
There's a joke book I've read
and a cook book, too.

Roses are fed
Violins play a tune

I'm not in bed
when the clocks say noon
Rose rockets will launch
as I eat lunch
It's a music munch
that rose with red rhyme.
I drink the red punch
so my powers come in a bunch.
I'm a Hayes with a hunch
and knowledgable kindness.

Walker Hayes
Columbia, MO

Love

Love is a very strong emotion,
especially when you have lots
of warmth and devotion.

God, family, and friends can
bring you happiness. None of us
wants anything less.

Jean, my love, and I were married
sixty-two wonderful years. We loved each
other dearly. I pray my family can find the
same happiness.

I hope as a family
we can stay close and be always
there for each other, even
when they are across
the country.

From west to east, north to south,
that's what families should be
all about—loving—like Jean was
with her family.

Charles Rodriguez
West Palm Beach, FL

War

It started under the warmth of the sun
Then an outbreak of people screaming one by one.
With a roar like that of thunder
Began the shadows of the sounds of laughter.

Is it over? Surely not, for the sound of war had only begun.
Families taking shelter desperately clinging to each other.
Men in outfits so peculiar started to point at one another;
With eyes of a hunter, they began to chase those trying to run.

Some tried to beg and barter for their lives;
Others tried their best just to hide.
But these strange men do not care;
They will find you—run if you dare!

However, not all will face this wave of mass genocide.
Unfortunately for some they will be forgotten in the rubble.
No doubt the tales will be told of the peril,
But some escaped to the countryside and carried on with their lives.

As time goes on the keys to the past rest with the living;
Yet it is so easy to forget what war can bring.

Breanna Ray
Sheridan, OR

There Was a Time

There was a time not so long ago.
The air was pure and the Earth was whole.

Families toiled from dawn to dusk.
Lived by the "Word" and simple trust.

The kitchen table was the highest court.
Open to complaints and a place to report.

The hallway candle wept waxen tears
And gave up its self to light the years.

The old ways faded and loosened the core.
Change was eminent, banging on the door.

The winds of time blew out the flame
When the incandescent brought Edison fame.

The mind of man opened an evolution;
That ignited the Industrial Revolution.

Harnessed on the back of an iron train,
Spread it west from city to plain.

Around the world it quickly traveled,
Leaving in its wake a climate unraveled.

Tess J. Wilke
Durand, IL

The Spiritual Moment

Happy in the moment I gazed
Heavenwards the blue sky.
My heart felt the spirit from on high.

God's presence was nigh.
I thought, whose child am I?

One of God's children was rejoicing.

I was content in "The Spiritual Moment."

Jewelean Taylor
McKenzie, TN

Untitled

How many people
does God place upon our paths
to alter our lives?
Each serves a unique purpose
to fulfill His master plan.

Joan Patterson Yeck
Moosic, PA

I wrote this poem because I feel so blessed to have wonderful people in my life. I thank God every day for the unconditional love and support of my family and friends. Our daughter Nicole taught me how to write different forms of poetry that she learned in a writing class at school. Since Nicole passed away three years ago, writing poetry brings me comfort and brings back memories of writing with her. I appreciate the opportunity to share my poems with others through your beautiful books. I enjoy reading the wonderful poetry of others.

The Reality of the Fairytale

People constantly chase real happiness.
They often mistake happiness as a
Materialistic thing. The goodness
Of this thing called happiness is the way
The satisfaction feels when you've found it.
The unfortunate thing is people ache
Because of this out-of-sight contentment.
Some even abandon this life and part.
They try and find prosperity elsewhere
Which this only brings anguish to others.
Why cause problems for a simple farewell?
Loathe themselves and wish to be another.
Happiness is a frightening matter,
But don't be anxious to find the answer.

Victoria Nichole Guerra
Tolleson, AZ

The Kings of a City

A lot of children loved Mr. Rogers
He was from the Pennsylvania city of Latrobe
So was the golf Pro Arnie Palmer
His outcome was a fantastic atropos

Mr. Rogers was an ordinary minister
His love for children was shown on his show
Arnies Army was not at all sinister
His love for golf was all he had to know

The banana split was also invented here
What a void it really filled
Many people can remember where
The ice cream sundae was finally killed

This city was built for these kings
All the people loved them so
The day came when they all set wings
They all were quite a big dynamo

Ronald Twardowski
Latrobe, PA

The Crooked Mile

Cold, lonely, feeling lost, empty and useless,
They would not allow me in.
"I walked the crooked mile."
I watched the people come and go,
The bright lights shining within where I could not go.
"I walked the crooked mile."
Unworthy, my clothes were tattered and torn,
Alcohol on my breath, holes in my shoes.
They said you cannot enter.
"I walked the crooked mile."
In my pain and suffering I cried out to the Lord.
He sent me an angel that night in the mist of my sorrow.
He showed me His loving kindness, mercy, and compassion.
He changed my life that night. One year later I spoke to sons
Of the angel God sent. I stopped them on the street, I asked
Do you remember me? They replied NO! I said
"I was the alcoholic in the park. Your mother brought me
three sandwiches, coffee, and a blanket.
I cried out to the Lord that night and he sent me an angel,
"your mother." My life changed that night.
"I no longer walked the crooked mile"

Roberta A. King
Albia, IA

Ruth Played Ball

He brought his bat
She came with a glove
He tried to steal
A little bitty kiss
But he struck out
She made him miss
He got a free pass
When he took a walk
She said it's not fair
He missed the chalk
Yes it was way foul
When he tried to score
She shut him out
And slammed the door
Was he flying out deep
About to miss the catch
Get those muscles loose
Work out and stretch
Don't get picked off
Take a shorter lead
With your next pitch
Better beg and plead
Then he hit a homer
With a walk-off run
He gave her a diamond
Calling Ruth (Babe) and won

Marvin Hitzemann
Waterloo, IL

White Flight

White
Pure
Illuminations
Sun beam
How I feel
Freedom revealed
My head raised
Looking above your flight
I feel I see soaring
Squinting to see
Fly, fly, fly
Until gone from view
I no longer see
Sight, sightless
Freedom flies
High above the sky
Fly, flying free
White flight flying above
Flyer you are
Spellbound, mystic
Two wings raised henched
Destination high
You see the face of the giver
Who feeds birds
Oh! White dove
Tell what his FACE reveals.

Khoda L. Stone
Louisville, KY

Power of Love

The power of love
Can heal all things
A hurt or neglected child
An abused woman
An abused man
Or an abused animal
Love is the one thing
That can help anyone or anything
Being able to trust in that after being hurt
Is the hardest thing to do
So start by trusting yourself again
By believing in yourself and loving yourself
Know that you are enough
That you are worthy of love
That you are strong enough
To stand on your own two feet
Be proud of the person you are
Don't let the negativity bring you down
You are beautiful
You are smart
You are creative
Most importantly you are loved

Chevelyn Curtis
Arnoldsville, GA

My Current Situation

I can't control or restrain
when my mind sends impulses in vain.
It's a hard illness to understand
because it seems to take you to another land.
Before a seizure you find yourself
questioning reality as it appears itself,
then it's almost like you float away
with no time, no space, or any idea of the day.
When you come back to reality,
memories of what you did no longer be.
Sometimes it's just of the time you were gone
or it may precede so far you become withdrawn.
Can't remember the first time you held your child...
Can't remember the first time she smiled...
It breaks your heart each and every day -
there has to be a reason, a why, or a way.
You can't do the things you used to do -
drive, socialize or act without falling through.
The only people you have are family
And you wonder how often you're considered an anomaly.
The one who has the most problems
When it started with one and slowly blossomed.
Yet, they still don't understand
How that person that had everything planned
Can't keep it together for just a little while
Without leaving reality, being sad, or acting hostile.

Melissa Kennedy
Little River, SC

I have been dealing with epilepsy for over a decade now. It is a very misunderstood and debilitating condition. It is important to note that my writing was my expression of my mind's comprehensive inner thoughts, not the judgment of my wonderfully supportive family. I would not be the woman I am today without their love and assistance.

I Wish

I wish I could be with you guys
Fighting beside you every day
Instead I'm here in Fort Living Room
Disabled and without my leg.

Thanks to every one of you
I'm alive and doing well.
It's still hard to deal with all of this;
I guess I'm in my own kind of Hell.

My right arm is paralyzed;
my right leg is gone.
But I try hard every day
to live my life and carry on.

So, my brothers,
keep your heads low;
this war will soon end.
When you get back home
look me up, my friends.

Kenneth L. Combs
Pahrump, NV

Green Dragon

The forces of heaven
And earth are a painter.
The paint is spilled over
The australis and borealis
Skies. The colors are constantly
Mixing and swirling to and fro
Together. As if this light
Were a living being.

As the painter swirls
His brush, different
Shapes are created
A green dragon forms
Over the frozen dark
Earth. No one wishes to
Slay this dragon but
All want to capture it.

They realize the dragon is
Only temporary; soon
The painter will swirl
His brush again, and
It will be gone. But for
Now it flies with it's wings
Outstretched, breathing
Stars instead of fire.

Carrie Carlton
Murfreesboro, TN

Great Artist

A farm boy want-to-be artist in NYC, no family and broke.
That was me, but I found my city stride, my Manhattan stroke.
Ignorant of subway's third rail, nearly struck by a bus, who'd care?
I visited Madison Square Garden, Coney Island, and Times Square.

Seeking a special destiny, I sought to develop the best in me.
Like a moth drawn to light, I flew a pattern of crazy flight.
The church said be humble, yet I set my goals high.
Pride precedes a tumble, still I wished to be a great artist, no lie.

Money—the root of all evil—a sign on the church steeple.
I memorized that rule then enrolled in a fine art school.
I studied El Greco, Van Gogh, and Dali. I learned anatomy and form.
Was my quest to be great pure folly? State of mind out of the norm?

My heart was skipping a beat; to continue would be a feat.
For love of art I'd self-deny. I'd go hungry, sleepless, even die.
With graduation looming, I'd soon end my art schooling.
I went on, stubborn as a goat, holes in my shoes and no coat.

In time, my fear of pride led to no art exhibited.
Money—as the root of all evil—would also lead to no sales.
Obviously I was psychologically inhibited.
Lacking sleep, I saw purple and yellow-green snails.

Slowly, I renounced the church of St. Holey Moley.
Post resignation, was I headed for hell-fire-damnation?
Now with a large corpus of work and nowhere to stow it,
I sit with brush in hand—a great artisan.

But, gee-willikers, only I know it.

Willi Wolfschmidt
Tucson, AZ

Glazed Reverie

Smoke spiraled from the incense, whimsy.
Boxes everywhere, running like a gypsy.
Standing on the roof garden,
Slightly past the horizon,
Discovered quick,
A beauty I share a light with.
Pass it on and step back.
As we fade into the band on deck.
I love to get down; so does she.
Marveling as she hoops beneath the willow tree.
Wonky eyes and vials, hair slips down her spine for miles.
Euphoria transcends.
A body that makes the heart descend.
As our night progresses the rest of humanity is restless.
In stillness sleeps chaos. A dream so heinous.

Amanda Patricia Arnold
Madison, WI

The author is a twenty-six-year-old poet and painter of nine years. She fell in love with the aesthetic of words after reading Jim Morrison's autobiography Nobody Here Gets out Alive. *From then on, it's been an addiction and a platform that's allowed her to grow through the human condition.*

Favorite Time of Year

Tis my favorite time of year
So I had better get in gear

Get out the festive tree
To that I do agree

Find the strings of lights
Which certainly could take some might

Where did I put the Christmas balls
Perhaps I left them in the hall

What about the Christmas Village
I had better do some major pillage

A really nice thing about those lights
They truly are nice and bright

Can't even find those pretty cards
Oh my that is becoming hard

The weather is turning cold
Surely turned out to be bold

So better get out the gloves
To wear while watching the doves

Ginger Garrett
Easton, MO

Christmas, Up North

The first snow of the season
is just so pleasin.'
It's like angel's wings so white and pure,
Mother Nature's hand at work, for sure.

Let's put up the tree
and call friends over to see.
We'll all make cookies
and share a cup of tea.

The carolers are singing in the street:
people are greeting people wherever you go.
The ice skaters are putting on a good show.
Ho, ho, ho, we hear Santa coming through the snow.

Friends and family gather near
with gifts of peace, love and cheer
to last us all through the year.

We go to church and say our prayers,
and sing a Christmas song or two.
Thanks be to our Lord,
another year, He has seen us through.

Barbara L. Page
Silver Bay, MN

Autumn Images

Like old, worn, tattered garments
Shriveled leaves lie strewn
In random patterns on the cold ground—
Dying sentinels awaiting the
Next frosty invasion.
Scattered flowers—faded remnants
Of summer's past glory
Peep furtively through crusty, crinkled
Foliage.
Covered with a light snow,
They attempt to perform summer's
Final show.
The waning autumn sun
Offers little assurance of continuing
Warm, bright garden days.
Reluctantly, the once gaily attired
Vibrant blooms
Surrender to the season's demands.
A lone rose struggles to maintain
Its summer radiance,
But beauty is fading and the rose
Will soon become one with the crusty,
Crinkled foliage surrounding it.

Stan A. Mendrick
Branchburg, NJ

At What Moment

At what moment
    does the present become the past
Never realizing what we cherished
    can never last

At what moment does one
    so loved in times passed
    become a precious memory
Never realizing what we cherished
    can never last

The past envelopes us
    Refuses to leave
Enmeshes with present thoughts
    into a suffocating weave

We dwell in lost hours of youth
    with feelings of happiness and pain
Clinging forever
    to a past that must remain

Yet where in time
    is this invisible line
    that makes the past seem
    a moment in a dream

A lifetime of long ago
    of tender memories passed
Never realizing what we once cherished
    can never last

Rhoda Needlman
Setauket, NY

Aleppo, Don't Cry...

Destiny's blow reduced you
To a wounded bird in agony;
Your eyes reveal a soul
Facing the stormy seas
Of demise... my Aleppo!
As the foe violated your borders,
They soiled your pride in self and country
By silencing your cathedrals' tolling bell towers,
Your holy mosques where the muezzins call,
Der Zor's holy mausoleum's sacred relics,
Remnants of my martyred forebears...
Oh horror of horrors!
Shelling, bombing, burning,
Day after day, week after week, month after month,
Year after year of hateful violence,
By predatory foes, native, and foreign...
Your wounded Citadel of many millennia
Rising above the city's dimmed lights,
Is commanding you to rise!
Soar high my crucified Aleppo!
The grandchildren of the genocidal death march
Are there, ready to alleviate your pain,
As you took the pain to shelter and sustain,
Their hopeless moribund grandparents,

During the Armenian Genocide's
Darkest final days...

Rosemarie Akian
Belleville, NJ

Rosemarie Maljian/Akian published her first short fiction novella Les Lueurs Sombres de la Destinee in 2011, in French under the pseudonym Ambear with Edilivre Editions APARIS. It was written in 1958–1959 after she completed her baccalaureate and her degree in philosophy. By 2013 she had translated into English as The Dark Glow of Destiny and she independently published it. Ambear returned to us in 2017 with her Unwilted Bouquet, a collection of Armenian and English poetry based on love, spirituality, history, nationalism, philosophy, and family memoirs.

Puissance

Breathe, celebrate our ways; never forget them.
Rejoice in the power of our forefathers and foremothers.
Puissance in each footstep.
Celebrate their words; sing loud, spirited.
Sing to the moon which they saw.
Sing to the stars which were in their eyes.
Rejoice in every step, tap the earth. Wake up old souls!
Let them know that we are still here, willing.
Dance, laugh; tell them that you will never stop;
never until we dance, laugh and shout together.
Always; still today; under HIS Eyes; never parted, never will.

Catherine Johnson Broussard
New Orleans, LA

Not Alone Did I Walk the Forest

Not alone did I walk the forest,
For darkness walked with me;
Until a sun-white butterfly
Came by and waved to me.

Wayne Newberry
Barrett, MN

One day as I was driving on a lonely, deserted back road, I encountered swarms and swarms of white butterflies. I have always liked butterflies and consider them to be signs of beauty and peace in nature. It is no wonder that a group of butterflies is called a kaleidoscope, for that is what they seem to be—nature's kaleidoscopes. I had no one with me to share the pleasure of this experience; I thus felt compelled to write about it. Beauty needs to be shared.

Looking for Spring, Jesus!

Oh my how sweet the light has begun.
Sun out a cool breeze to please.
Our redbud also dogwood explode in the woods.
The air is filled with the fragrance of cut grass.
Smile, we're all ready for spring.
New life has sprung;
come, come adore the growing season.
Seed, soil, and water produce a harvest to please:
red tomatoes, yellow squash, and the fat round watermelons.
Oh please we look to Jesus, the Master, you see.
He chose spring to come again, my friend.
There the fig tree branch has already become tender
and put forth its leaves.
Look up, summer is near.
When you see a rainbow of colors
recognize that He is near right at the door.
Look up, it's spring.
For many years I have thought it significant that Jesus
chose a spring image to signify the end of age.
Still so, in the mist of the woods
the dogwood blooms.
Let's always remember though, His Son Jesus Christ.
God prepares a new Heaven and a new Earth!
Spring and summer are coming!

Francis Dianne Solomon
Corsicana, TX

I was born March 28, 1956, and I am from Lubbock, TX. I work as a fitness center supervisor and in my spare time I enjoy reading, writing, word finds, puzzles, cards, and drawing cartoons. I've been married for forty-eight years and have four children. I love to listen then respond on a subject going forth. Our words do really matter. The truth unfolds. Open your eyes and heart and you will see.

The History of Love

For human beings, love started with Adam and Eve
Passed between generations for you and me

I want love to grow through our children and kin
I want love to blossom, continue till this world ends

The history of love began with time
It was made for every man, woman, and child

Love is the way we express that we care
It is more than having an affair

There are deep emotions for the one you are involved
You show them by saying, I need you around

The history of love will continue if we want it that way
It will last forever, let's start today

Myles Wallace
Chicago, IL

Ever True Ever Blue

What can I say, as I listen
My heart skips a beat
For another hero dressed in blue has fallen
I shed many a tear for I live in fear
For each and every day, for someone to say
Oh God, why must they pay
For the evil that lurks
And never seems far away
The men and women who risk their lives
To keep us safe
Like guardian angels up on high
They rush towards danger, and have no fear
That their lives
May be only a breath away
From unshed tears
Loved ones who hope and wait
That they never hear
Those hateful words
That love of duty has called them home

Marie E. Belensky
Taylor, PA

This poem in a small way is a thank you for all the men and women who face danger every day and put their lives on the line. Their duty is to protect and keep us safe. May God watch over you and keep you safe from harm.

Beholder

Look!
Look what the horizon holds,
Sentinels of the past.
See!
See thee epic that unfolds
Far beyond our grasp!
Listen!
Listen to the sounds of peace
That is forever here!
Hear!
Hear our soul's fears release
Into this new frontier.
Feel!
Feel life's eternal bliss
That still remains at hand.
Scence!
Scence thee almighty kiss
Of the power that will stand!
Forever!
Forever keep in mind this scene
Of glory days gone by.
Always!
Always know that unforseen
Is that special beauty to thee eye.

Clay Thompson
Pocatello, ID

"Beholder" is a poem I wrote for the beauty of "Craters of the Moon" national monument. The "standing dead" trees reminded me of sentinels guarding nature's beauty. I grew up exploring the Great Rift Monument in Idaho. I have always been amazed by standing dead trees and their beauty and grace.

His Name Was Ricky

There were many like him,
in those days gone by,
dedicated men, trained to a razor's edge,
ready to fly, to any point on the globe,
in their swift weapons of war.
The call could come at any time, day or night,
and they would be off,
to face the unknown.
To those who knew and loved him,
he was more than a crewman
on a complicated bomber,
he was a good friend and team member,
husband, and father of three.
His devotion to his job
in the service of his country,
was beyond question.
His family, whom he cherished,
still misses him, and always will.
The tragic mishap that ended his short life
should never have happened,
but it did,
and the void it left
can never be filled.

Steven M. Lambert
Warwsaw, IN

My poem honors a young air force airman, Capt. Manuel "Rocky" Cervantes, who perished on December 8, 1964 when his fuel-laden B-58 bomber exploded in flames on the runway. Rocky attempted to escape the flaming bomber by ejecting via his escape pod since the B-58 was surrounded by a literal wall of fire. His pilot weapons systems officer had managed to leap from the aircraft to safety. Upon ejection, Rocky, in his escape pod, was hurtled approximately 400 ft. From the bomber to land hard in the snow. He was mortally injured and died an hour later at the base hospital on Bunker Hill AFB, Indiana (later to be renamed Grissom AFB). Capt. Rocky Cervantes was survived by his wife and three young children. He was twenty-nine years old.

Behind Enemy Lines

When the enemy comes in his cause is very clear;
His only option is to destroy your very will.
It doesn't happen suddenly;
He takes his time to corrupt your mind.
You become blinded and the truth begins to bend.
You are unaware that you have let the enemy in.
People around you can see that you have been displaced,
But you are lost in the sin
That will soon become your disgrace.
The lies begin to grow, and your fate is most certain
If you don't turn and walk away.
The enemy is crafty and doesn't want to let go,
But the God inside of you knows the truth
Hidden deep inside your heart.
So, He releases the angels and charges them this day,
To surround you with protection
And show you the error of your ways.
You fall down broken and awaken to your call;
You rise up a mighty warrior ready to fight for all!

Cheri Tharp
Sugar Creek, MO

God is first in my life and helps me to share the things I have gone through with poems. Pain doesn't have to last if you learn to let go and let God, then He will take care of the rest. Situations should not define you; they should be learning experiences that take you to the next level.

Yoshi

He came as a reject.
At 12 weeks, 8 pounds, unwanted,
he was sent on his way.
Blessings come hard;
sometimes, they are scarred.
Boisterous and outgoing,
no one understood.
When he swings,
the house rings.
Sometimes I reminisce,
who would castoff
a life such as this?
Outrageous, highly intelligent, full of curiosity,
he came with gentle simplicity.
His loving nature had never been realized.
His personality was stylized.
Mr. Transport Man came and
handed me a squirming pup.
Bye Mr. Transport Man; thanks for the ride.
The little guy instantly snuggled into my arms
somehow knowing he was home—forever.
What more could you ask
of this charming young captor?

Bonnie Culver
Fritch, TX

A friend of mine had rescued an unwanted pregnant Japanese Chin. Four pups were born, three boys and a girl. The baby girl died soon after birth. The remaining three boys were adopted. I took one called Andy. Two and a half weeks later, my friend called wanting to know if I would take Yoshi because his adopter didn't want him. The excuse given, he wasn't house broke and he didn't pay attention. I'm now the proud mama of twin boy pups. Andy is conservative and Yoshi is adventurous.

Without the Lights On

It is dark
in that lonely hovel
at night without the lights on
surrounded by the cobwebbed glory of the past
which can never change.
Anger opening up like that top
that once popped, let out a sizzle.
One sip,
then two,
guzzling up that healing brew,
staring hopelessly into that gaping black mouth
of a worthless ten cents.
One tear,
then two,
a sniffle
as she fingers that smooth, aluminum surface.

Her angry regrets expressed
through the amber-colored tears
drunk alone
in that silent hovel.
At night.
Without the lights on.

Meghan Elizabeth Sonder
Montague, MI

I like to get a sense of the human element, putting myself in the shoes of another to get an idea of what it must be like. There is a beauty in understanding even the darkest elements of human existence and that is what I enjoy the most about my writing.

Why Is Love Important?

I think love has great significance.
It's something you can't touch, hold, or sell,
so why do we need it then?
Love is something I'm not able to define well.
It gives us hope that we need.
It's something you can't fake.
It's knowing someone is loyal and won't leave;
it's a bond you can't break.
I'm always grateful that there is always love for me.
Love is something everyone should be.
Love is loyal, strong, kind, and everlasting,
so why is this the thing everyone is lacking?
Soon love will be no more,
then everyone's hearts would be sore.
Because love would be close to non-existent;
everyone would hate and want to be distant.
So we should appreciate and love
before our time is up and we are sent above.

Mieko Takeshima-Price
Rialto, CA

I think love is something people disregard sometimes, and we're not grateful for the things we have. We don't always appreciate the little things people do for us. I just wanted to bring some insight as someone fortunate enough to experience love from my close family and friends regularly. What inspired me to write this poem is the way I view love, and I wanted to share this with more people. I wanted to inspire more people to be aware of love in their lives.

Little Hands

Little hands small and warm
Hold my hand so close
Sweet little fingers tickle
my nose; so much love they show.
Growing fast, holding tight,
so much to learn.
From little hands my child grows
into a fine young man.

Jeannie C. Smith
North Little Rock, AR

Water Within

Submersed in sacred waters floating and
freely unwinding; I feel my own current pulling
at the depth of my being. The waves within
me playing with the bubbles of enlightenment.
The pebble of this blessing creates a ripple of
1000 dreams. Of fin and feather I fly
or float in tune with all abound. My substance
has been rearranged and I find I am not
the same, when my feet come down and
touch the ground.

Julia M. Meno
Cornwall Bridge, CT

Planet Earth and the human body both share the same percentage of water within our mass. An aquatic therapist and adventurer, I see the profound healing properties of water almost daily. The power and grace of water always inspires me.

The Sum of Its Parts

If I was a sculpture,
I would pick up that broken muffler,
the one abandoned on the corner of Carter Street & Hickory Drive.
I'd don a welding hood and give it arms and legs.
Born would be a tin man.
Or a carpenter who after storms, collects the downed trees,
slicing them up to create tables and chairs.
Conversation ringing in the years of drought, flood, and bitter cold
New England winters.
After two frozen weeks without power,
electricians traveled from Quebec to
re-ink black-pen lines upon our winter sky.
They wore headphones and danced,
celebrating as they composed in current verses.
Tapping the icy streets with music that buzzed from ears to feet.
In a halting, broken puzzle of French I offered coffee to the workmen.
A tiny spark of warmth I could conjure with my newly reconnected volts.
The men swapped their own broken words with mine.
Merci non, off in search of a bottle of whiskey.
Sea glass. Driftwood. Trees and people fairly trading CO_2 and O_2.
Babies, with mountains of paperwork,
brought across the city or the ocean, to make a family whole.
A hand, found and clasped.
That sublime satisfaction of finding pieces that fit.

Juliet Grinnell Howe
New Canaan, CT

Recently, I tried to give my husband and myself a welding class as an anniversary gift. Sadly, the class was already full. We were both disappointed. That same week, I spied a muffler by the side of the road and "Sum of Its Parts" and not an actual Tin Man was born. I often see things as they might be, but am amazed by the way the world seems to work itself out and keep spinning. Juliet Howe is a graduate of Skidmore College, a poet, singer, gardener and storyteller. She lives in Connecticut with her husband and three children.

The Stages of Home

Home started on the block, crocker way
Home turned to trouble those were the bad days
Home was nana talk on the rougher days
The day she passed stole all that away
The rainy days are not here to stay
Home was green grass on the field, those were greater days
Home wasn't always a place more often than not.
Home was a short blonde that stole my heart
Home was another heartbeat, home was a soul far greater than mine, that home is no longer my concern
Now home is a distant place a place that misses many things
Home will always be locked within the walls of you're heart
Until home decides that you don't deserve to be home anymore.

Dante Matthew Kukula-Briggs
Centennial, CO

My name is Dante. I am twenty-one and currently serving in the US Army on active duty. Lost love inspired me to create this poem, and it is my favorite piece so far.

The Pine Tree

As I stretch my arms to the sky,
Finally touching the heavens nearby.
My green needles poke at the air,
While I drop some brown needles off there.
I live happily through the day and the night,
It's the nature I have to continually fight.
I'm just like you not satisfied,
On Mother Nature I relied.
In the winter I get too cold,
In the summer I seem to fold,
But there's the rain to make me bold,
Strengthening my roots becoming a stronghold.
Every year it's like this to me,
Continually sowing beauty for thee.

David P. King
Falmouth, MA

I was born in Bakersfield, CA in 1954. My mother's father was an accomplished writer and travelled the world sharing his books. My father's mother was also an accomplished writer and shared her books with others. Most of my aunts and uncles were writers and artists. Among my immediate family of brothers and sisters, a lot of poetry was written. I have been writing since I learned to write at age six. I was inspired to write this poem as I observed the many varieties of pine trees in a neighborhood I lived at in West Hyannisport, MA. The pine tree is used for so many things around the earth and is considered the most commercialized plant and product I know of.

The North Winds Blow Strong

In the North where we met, that land of deep forests,
Where the sun stays up late to make long summer days,
The nights are all magic with northern lights dancing,
And folks keep their word, and respect the old ways.
There we met and I loved you, and you gave me children,
And they grew up strong, but then you had to go;
You fought hard to stay, and I fought hard to keep you,
Until your worn body released its strong soul.

In the North where we lived, that land of deep winters,
Where day leaves early to make long winter nights;
There, the magic still lives in a house that is lonely;
I still honor my promise; its burden is light.
No, I cannot leave you alone in this forest,
For the promise I made is so easy to keep.
The North Winds blow strong in the forest this evening,
Chasing leaves all around at the place where you sleep;
And I wish you were with me; yes, I wish we could go,
To the places where the wild North Winds blow...

Lowell Grant Gill
Temperance, MI

I am sometimes moved to develop a poem on a matter that has popped into my head out of nowhere. As writing begins, I have no idea how it originated, where it's going, or how it will end. This poem is an example of this unstructured process. However, as I read it for editing, I realized it was a condensed story of my mother and father. The muse is certainly interesting. I trust you will find it to be acceptable for your purpose. Thank you for considering me. Lowell G. Gill (also a proud veteran)

The End of the Road

As we approach the end of the road
It's impossible not to reflect on what should be told
All of life's journeys come into view
And it is now time, to tell all of you

Life has its pleasures, disappointments, too
Joys have been plentiful, sorrows few
Memories of kids and grandkids are a joy to recall
Watching you evolve has been the best of all

We are old, at the end of the road
As we go off into the sunset gold
Remember all you have been told
All we taught you, loved you, as you, too, grow old
And reach the end of the road.

Frances Richter
St. Louis, MO

I have always loved poetry and have written many poems for special occasions. I once wrote my husband a poem when we got married fifty-nine years ago. When your announcement was received, I thought about it and decided to write what is on my mind now . . . emotional times.

The Broken True Glass

She keeps busting his crystal ball.
He keeps trusting love conquers all.
He won't forgive. She won't forget.
They cannot live without regret.
He needs to know the past is past.
Then she can go in peace at last.
She needs to be set free of scorn.
Then he can see a brand new dawn.
He can't forgive. She can't forget.
How can they live without regret?

Glynn Holmberg
New York, NY

Love is what makes life worth living. Art is the genius born of love. Music is the art of the muse. Poetry is the language of love. During times of conflict, art can degenerate into a weapon of war. What was meant to be an aspect of love becomes an instrument of hate. When the conflict is over, things never go back to being the same. Even soothing music can be irritating when it triggers painful memories. For those who still feel threatened or offended, it is difficult to forgive or forget.

Tell Me the Names

What is the name
Of the child who died?
Were ICE'd parents notified?
Does anyone know where those parents reside?
What is the name
Of the tot who's dead?
Did anyone sit beside her bed?
Did anyone comfort his aching head?
What of the cage-mates
Trapped inside?
Who cared as they trembled,
Terrified?
Tell me the name of the child who died
The guards could not, if they even tried.
Tell me the name, each name, every name
Tell me the stone-cold who authored this game.
Open the gates, let the innocents flee
Lock up instead the heartless he
Who architected this infamy.
Tell me the names.

Corinne Whitaker
Carmel, CA

Corinne Whitaker, aka the Digital Giraffe, is the author of thirty books of poetry, a forty-one year pioneering digital sculptor and painter, and winner of two Golden Web awards for her digital giraffe eZine, now celebrating twenty-five years of monthly web publication (www.giraffe.com. She has exhibited worldwide in over 350 exhibitions and is the creator of a new iconography of vision for the digital era.

Sniffer

Santa has a wonder dog and Sniffer is his name.
Sniffer never did a thing to get him any fame.
He mostly sleeps everyday and sometimes hides a bone.
Each Christmas Day he gets to lick a drippy ice cream cone.
Sniffer only has one chore which he does once a year.
Santa sends old Sniffer out to round up all the deer.
He always finds all of them in time to pull the sleigh.
Without old Sniffer's hunting skills there's be no Christmas Day.
Sniffer really earned his keep one stormy Christmas Eve.
A blizzard was a blowing when he went to retrieve
The deer that Santa needed to pull the Christmas sleigh
Could not be found anywhere. No deer were at play.
Sniffer knew it was up to him to find all the deer.
Without them to pull the sleigh there would be no cheer.
There'd be no toys for Tommy or dolls for sister too.
Christmas would be canceled. Santa would be through.
Without Santa climbing in, bringing all the toys
There would be no Christmas for all the girls and boys.
So Sniffer had to use his nose to sniff out all the deer.
'Cause Christmas without Santa would be a thing to fear.
Sniffer finally got a scent of a polar bear
It now made him understand why no deer were there.
No deer was safe from the claws of such a mighty beast.
They ran to keep from being: the bear's Christmas feast.
As Sniffer sniffed, the scent grew strong. He was getting near.
Finally in blizzard snow he saw all the deer
Huddled in a giant herd – they were all on guard.
The bear was a circling round and round the yard.

Carl E. Sundberg
Sweet Home, OR

I am a retired man in my seventies. I write poems and songs of all kinds. After nearly five decades as a broadcast engineer, I have retired to a life sharing the joys of the golden years with my wife of forty-six plus years. I spend much of my time writing songs and poems and creating an engine to convert ocean heat into free electric power to power the planet while battling global climate change. My favorite poets are Poe and Vachel Lindsay. I love children and have written many poems for them. Next year I'll enter another epic Christmas poem that addresses two important questions about Santa.

Simply Beautiful

There are many different types of touch—a family touch,
a laughing touch, a friendly touch, a loving touch.

Have you ever enjoyed the very first touch of a man.
Most of the time, that very first touch
doesn't really mean much because he's just a friend.
But his *touch* was *simply beautiful*.

Have you ever enjoyed, the first time
he lightly touched your hand?
Or the way he softly stroked your arm.
Have you ever enjoyed someone's company
so much that it scared you?
Because he was only a friend—nothing else.

Has someone ever touched you
for the first time and made you feel things
you didn't really want to feel?
Or made you feel special, just by his touch?

Well, his touch was simply beautiful.
Just a simple touch . . . and I enjoyed it.

Carol D. Brewer
Pomona, CA

I've been writing poetry for about forty-five years, mostly about love. I'm a hopeless romantic. I'm seventy-one years old, and I have a great life. Urban ballroom dancing keeps me moving. I've been dancing for almost five years, and I love it. I love decorating, planning parties, spending time with my family and my senior lady friends, whom I lovingly call, "Silly Seniors." This poem was written on August 6, 2019 and was inspired by my friend Tom Ross. As a group, we went out to celebrate his birthday, and this is what happened—he touched me (smile).

Seek Him

Find God in all that you do
Stay on track, to what is true
Look to the Lord for hope
As you daily cope
In all the strife
That consists of life

Find rest in His arms
Kept away from the harms
Trust in the risen Jesus, the Lord
Who died for our sins and restored
All of us to Him, whom we adore
And love so much more

Empress Kelly
Lake Havasu City, AZ

Empress Kelly was born in South Korea. She was adopted and raised in the United States. Kelly writes worship poetry to bring Jesus and God to the minds of her readers. It is her hope that her poetry will bring the readers to faith in Jesus as Savior. "Seek Him" is about how we have the opportunity every day to go to God for counsel and help. You can follow Kelly on twitter @byEmpressKelly.

Peaceful Beings

Intelligent people proclaim that we are peaceful beings.
Perhaps there is something about us that they are not seeing.
We don't see ourselves as animals, but that is what we are.
Take a long look at human behavior, from near or afar.
Our blind attraction to the absurd causes atrocities.
We maim and kill our own species with mindless ferocity.
A volcanic rage lies deep inside us, ready to erupt.
It is there to be released by the malicious and corrupt.
Our insecurities lead us to blame others for our fate.
Vicious people know how to manipulate that into hate.
We fear making painful life changes necessary for survival.
We see others, not as welcomed friends, but as ruthless rivals.
Our boundless cruelty surpasses that of all known predators.
The poisonous venom of pure hatred oozes from our pores.
What is the source of such dreadful and horrifying evil?
Some say there are demons who cause us deep psychic upheaval.
We can't defend against such powerful external forces.
If so, we may see those dreaded apocalyptic horses.
Most likely, nature imbued us with evil capacity.
That idea comes from best science, not cold audacity.
Will evolution change humans so that in peace we may dwell?
Or will we annihilate ourselves and the planet as well?
As mother earth is obliterated there will be no sound.
Evidence of our futile existence will never be found.
A silent universe will not mourn what we foolishly lost.
Yes, if we remain hate-filled, we will bear a horrendous cost.

LeRoy F. Thielman
Oshkosh, WI

It is an undeniable fact: We have annihilated hundreds of millions of our fellow human beings. Shamefully, it appears we are planning to kill millions more. Yet, it is difficult to comprehend and to accept that all human beings have the capacity for evil. Ignoring that fact has devastating cruel consequences. We are the good guys and they are the "evil-doers." That is our evolutionary perspective. But before we attempt to exorcise evil from others, we need to learn how to subdue our own. With those disturbing thoughts reverberating in my mind, I wrote the poem, "Peaceful Beings."

One Wish

If I had one wish what would it be
Wealth, health, or more stuff?
When I think of all those things,
True happiness they don't bring.
We all want wealth! We need our health!
Do we think what does God want for us?
We go to church, we pray
We still don't know at the end of the day.
We want so much, all God wants for us is to trust;
He gives us joy and peace
When all we have we release.
All the stuff that means so much,
We can't take with us when God we touch.

JoAnn Shackleford
Lawrenceville, GA

I am an eighty-seven-year-old widow. All my poetry is inspired by my faith, a gift from God to share with others. "One Wish" was inspired by how we wish and want so much and less of God. My writing brings me much joy.

My Journey

My world is such a different place—
What happened to the sunshine?
What happened to the smiles no longer on my face?

Without my love I'm no longer whole—just half.
My pain cries out! I feel its wrath!

Tears, like rain, are flowing in my soul.
Happiness escapes me—will I ever again feel whole?

My love now rests in peace, but my sadness remains
refusing to cease!

I hate how my life has changed.
It's wearing to always feel drained.

I truly am trying but it's hard going on.
The days drag by; the nights are so long.

Gradually pushing through my fog I feel
slight waves of peace and thin rays of hope.

Could my prayers be answered? Could, maybe,
just maybe, I'll learn how to cope?

Charlene K. Heim
Haven, KS

I, like many others, have recently lost the love of my spouse through death. The journey through grief each of us must travel is unique to each individual, but the emotions we feel are often very common. My poem "My Journey" is my feelings as I traveled the long grief journey. Perhaps it may speak to others.

My Heart

A song; fire glowed in
Colored streaks
Rich harmony speaks
A soft poem tuck away
To bring out when needed
For a smile someday
A stay sentence trudges along
Wrapped in thoughts.
Shelter in warmth, of a song,
was caught.
Surrounded presence to feel,
Unique and real.
A song might be in disguise,
Make it increasingly wise.
A song's a faithful friend.
Around when each silver,
Note has ascends.
Invite one in your heart,
for since it dwells within.

Connie R. Holt
Waynesboro, TN

"Song in My Heart" is gratefully dedicated to my grandchildren; their bright minds and yards of imagination inspired its creation. For my husband Marvin, just because I love him.

My Father Would Say

My Father would say
Buy quality; cry once
His subtle lessons
Then there is no shame
He would walk in his Romeo slippers
Along the street by our home
Always giving advice and listening
Always listening
To his thoughts and my prattle
Do what you like to do least, first, then you will
Have the freedom to do what you want
He would inspect the street at his feet
Give his silent approval
Never be afraid to ask a foolish question
He walked with his hands clasped behind his back
Comfortable long strides
His leather soles against the sand
Don't let a stranger's words hurt you, they don't know you
He would walk on in silence
Gentle soul

Ellen E. Hildebrand
Sheboygan, WI

I lost my father when I was nineteen years old. I still think of our walks and his lessons to me. He was a giant of a man at 5'10"; he was my knight in shining armor.

Mira

I look for you everywhere-
and can't find you.
Sound of a voice—
a laugh—
makes my heart think
there you are!
and it's not.
Not you. Never you.
So I continue
to look for you-
in the memories
living within me-
touch of your hand
soft brush of your lips
strength of your hug
gentleness of your caring.
I can always find you
in the memories
living in my heart.

Maggi Wright
San Jacinto, CA

This poem was written for my David—the one who brought me out of the darkness and back into the light! My heart is yours forever. I have always enjoyed writing poetry. Started writing poems when I was six years old. I have written about love, wonder, sadness...all the emotions a person feels! I like to watch as someone reads what I have written and guess what they are feeling! Expressions are my greatest critic!

Old Age

Goodness gracious, golly gee,
How do you expect to see
Without glasses? Pray tell.
When your eyes are aging? Well?
You need a cane to help you stand,
When your knees no longer bend.
Your teeth are not your own.
False teeth, now you own.
Your hair is silver or white
Age plays its tricks, O delight!
If you hear, it's a miracle
course, now, be practical
Old age, time has flown
your time, years have blown.

Mildred E. Frazier
Urbana, OH

James Moss

James Moss fried fish in
the brown skillet
A pinch of salt
A sprinkle of Old Bay
A dusting of corn meal
Flipped once, flipped twice
Fried till golden brown
Placed on two of Hattie's old plates
Eaten with two hands, a fork
and hot sauce.

Victor Brown
Atlanta, GA

Augustus Calvin Brown Jr. (Macon, GA) 1932 and Lovata Moss Brown (Edgecomb, NC) 1932. Victor Brown, BA Lemoyne Owen College, Memphis, TN, 1989.

In the Potter's Hand (Prayer)

You are the potter, I am the claythe vessel in use feels great dismay.
The crack is getting wider and more porous-liethe sparks from
the fire getting hot with intensity.

OH Lord ,I seem to be in a jagged hole
muddy ,dirt, stones snakes with morbid old moles.
My nourishment came from a little brown mug
and you pored the sweetest brew in that cup.

 HAIL TO THE KING who's watching ore' me,a touch from the
master's hand so tender and sweet. I know this too will pass,
as we talk one on one,walking side by side as we cross the pond,

Over the bridge which was made for me,
Jesus opened my eyes to let me see
the lilies, which made the pond a living garden
for me to enjoy and receive great pardon.

 My child ,you are not alone as you think,
I have send people your way to be that link
between your sister and brother who are just a few,
just open your eyes and see the ready made crew.

Christel Decker Bresko
Medical Lake, WA

I was born in Germany in 1937 and am the eldest of three children. My father served in the German army until 1945, the year he became a prisoner of war after being captured in Moscow, Russia. I went to England in 1957 to study the English language while working as a nursemaid for an old lady with MS. There I received my nursing degree in 1962. In 1968 I came to the United States and started my family with my husband Bill. My world was disrupted in 2005 when my immune system fell apart and I was diagnosed with breast cancer. The joy of the Lord is my strength.

In a Magical Mountain Cabin

Where outside my window
Time stands still
And nothing seems
Real.

Peaceful and quiet
As snow drifts down
Turning everything in sight
Pure white.

The trees are covered
In snow
As the log on the fire
Burns low.

I take a walk
In the snow so deep
It crunches
Beneath my feet.

The world
Seems so clean
What
An awesome scene.

Just outside is a snowball fight
And winter fun
That could last into
The night.

Margaret Worley
Watertown, TN

This is the ninth time I've been published by Eber & Wein Publishing. I've been published six time by the International Society of Poets and have been in Noble House twice. I went to a writers school for two years at Institute of Children's Literature and Long Ridge Writer's Group. I had wonderful teachers at both schools. I love poetry, reading, the outdoors, and speak my opinions openly—all should have this right in this world. My writing has also been in newspapers, magazines, and CD tapes. God has made my world great and joyful. Thanks to Eber & Wein.

I'm Amazed, Oh Lord

I'm amazed oh Lord by your creation
Like an artist who creates a masterpiece on canvas
I'm amazed oh Lord by your masterpiece
Called Earth; You gave it light by the sun

And the moon to shine upon the earth at night
I'm amazed oh Lord your most priceless work
Of creation of man from dust of the earth and
And woman from the rib of man
I'm amazed oh Lord You created every living creature
Whichever roamed the earth from every form of bird
Whichever lived upon the earth throughout the ages

And filled the ocean's with every species of fish
I'm amazed oh Lord how you watered the earth and
All living things upon the earth
You brought forth the waters
From the depths of the abyss and made it all anew

I'm amazed oh Lord you painted the earth with the four
Seasons which the nations of the world depend upon
When to plant their crops and when to harvest

You set a time for life on Earth each in its own
Will return back to dust but oh Lord I'm amazed
You have provided a means of escape for mankind
From the abyss to a home in Heaven where
The soul never dies

Joe J. Espinoza
Glendale, AZ

I was inspired to write my poem "I'm Amazed Oh Lord" in hopes the reader will see a part of the Bible and that no else can claim the masterpiece of our Lord's creation; He is the author and finisher of our faith. "He is the Alpha and Omega, the beginning and the end, the first and the last." He has provided mankind a means to escape the grave to a home in Heaven where the soul never dies.

I Believe in Unicorns

I believe in unicorns and other magical things;
I believe that only you can shape what the future brings.

I believe in rainbows that hide a pot of gold;
I believe that each new day is big and bright and bold.

I believe that each dark cloud has a silver lining;
Try real hard and you will know the thrill that comes with winning.

I believe in pixie dust that makes my heart take flight,
And transforms my imagination far beyond my sight.

I believe in hidden gems and places to explore;
I believe I'll always take just that one step more.

I believe that I can sense what others never find;
The love and peace and happiness that's right inside my mind.

I believe in the joy I feel when your sweet voice sings;
I hope that I will always be the "wind beneath your wings."

I believe in unicorns for they make dreams come true;
I believe in all these things, most of all—I believe in you!

Tina Allen
Seminole, FL

I wrote this poem as part of a birthday gift for Grace, a very creative and talented former student of mine. This was written to inspire her to not become discouraged and to trust in her wonderful gifts and abilities. I encourage her to never give up and to keep reaching for her dreams and goals; someday she may reach her "unreachable star!"

High Clouds

You were there and I could see you
even with my eyes closed
covering up their natural blueness, while my
literal heart ached and longed for newness
from strain and fear, which I had thrown on it.
Poor heart! Poor you, to have to watch
me gasp and struggle, fighting against a mean
and dire danger to my soul! I inhaled steadily
but with urgency and exhaled smoothly through
O-shaped lips too pursed to smile at you.
You were there, too, when the danger waned
like when high clouds begin to fade, then fly off
our own sky! They allow brilliant sun beams
through the foliage of forests deeply green.
Oh, darkness can visit any one of us as a false
platform for our mind, to begin feeding anxieties
that will paralyze good actions we try.
So, this day I now behoove you—please stay
my best supporting fan, for this life; indeed,
I breathed my way back to it—unbloodied, not
even broken (a modern miracle). And
today I lift this toast of sweet, oxygenated air up
gratefully, ecstatically to you!

Virginia L. Kaplan
Salem, OR

"High Clouds" was inspired by an unexpected stay in the hospital, where it was found I had over an inch of fluid in my lungs. This made breathing extremely hard, and I was frightened. It was a life-threatening emergency circumstance which I had to fight hard to overcome. This poem honors my family's continual presence there with me. I believe my family members gave me strength and hope to heal; they are forever a part of who I am.

Heavenly Overture

Yon morning breaks through colors bold—
tangerine, magenta, mid-fluorescent gold.

Vaporous ribbons arise to greet
such splendor, blending in a symphonic suite.

As Del Sol's warmth dispels this sound,
deep azure back-drops, while white billows abound.

In this work-a-day world, minutes meld with a blur;
as with fast-acting watercolors, confusion may occur.

Lo, behold at day's end, our sky-palate returns,
Oft times more vibrant, e'en as bright as flame burns.

Too soon, the moon re-appears, stage right,
as curtains of stars ease the blackness of night.

Thus finishing our colorful overture of scenes,
we snuggle into night-clouds
for more technicolor dreams.

Rosemarr Greathouse
Carbondale, CO

Sadly, I have inherited my mother's family's macular degeneration, but luckily, I have responded well to the injections, which were not available for her. It was a family tradition for my sisters who lived close by to take our mom on a "Sunday alert" each evening. As time passed by, they would give her word descriptions of the colors. This poem is dedicated to my mom who would have been one hundred years old this October. She was also a poet.

Heaven Is Real

A long time ago when I was a little thing
I floated to the ceiling in the room I was in.
I saw myself lying on a bed but I wasn't alone;
There was a big angel there to take me home.

I don't remember the trip, just mostly the play.
Mountains with snow on them and warm as we sleighed.
Walking through flowers, beauty beyond compare;
No harm came to them and glorious music in the air.

A river crystal clear like living colors that flowed
If I had a question to ask, I suddenly seem to know
God's Presence surrounded me, so strong and safe and sure
Everything there was so beautiful, clean, holy, and pure.

Then Jesus said, I had to go back
As I looked into His eyes of love
I couldn't say no, but I didn't want to go,
Only to stay in this world above.

I had hoped my experience would help others someday
To let them know there is nothing to fear.
Your loved one has just moved and gone away
And it's more wonderful there than here.

Shalom Christina Zoë
Roswell, NM

The poem is true and others who have been there have confirmed what I experienced. There are mountains and trees; it's a lot like Earth. If you lost a child or had an abortion, God has them all up there. I just want people to realize that Heaven and Jesus is real, and the only way to Heaven is to get saved. Romans 10:9, 10 And since Heaven is real, so is the other place. Your spirit looks just like your body and your mind, will, and emotions go with you so you will remember your life on Earth.

Good Enough!

Do not visit that distant past,
the events of long ago,
painful as they might be,
are just that, "The Past."
Who you are today is not what you were then.
Notice please, the words who and what.
In the past, you were what others saw ... or not.
What they wanted you to be to fit their perception of you.
Who you are is who you wish to be,
who you believe you can be,
who makes you feel good to be you.

Remember above all else:
"Who you are is good enough!"
What you are can and will change throughout
your life.

Be who makes you proud!
Be what makes you happy!

"Who you are is good enough!"

Kathleen Forstner
Ashland, OR

I often hear people belittle themselves or feel down because others have belittled them and I was hoping to be able to put into words that we are all good enough! It is not that believing we are good enough makes us better than others, but to realize and internalize we are not less. Thank you and always remember, "Who you are is good enough!" Do your part and assure others they, too, are good enough. We all are!

Freedom Road

If all the world despises you
Yet, resolutely, you respect yourself
And thank God for the precious gift
of life bestowed
Then viscious slander will not
find its mark in you
And hatred will turn back upon itself
The masses will be silenced by
your fortitude
Dumbfounded by the beauty
of your grace
Your light will shine to show
the way to all who see
To those who live in darkness
and in dread
The way to freedom is the road
to Calvary
Where truth will banish fear
and lead you on
By giving up this life to gain
eternity.
Darkness vanquished
Hallelujah, comes the dawn.

Carol M. Heineman
Lehigh Acres, FL

Millions know the award-winning author of sixty crime novels Anne Perry. What some people may not know is that when she was sixteen years old she helped her best friend murder the friend's mother. They bludgeoned her to death—not exactly your typical what-I-did-last-summer essay. Going off to prison for five years she experienced firsthand the horrors of life behind bars. In her own words, in her utter brokenness, she fell to her knees and confessed her sins to God, accepting Jesus Christ as her Lord and Savior, and she was set free.

Fight This Battle

Oh, Lord my Lord
Fight, fight, and fight this battle
The battle that I'm in I need you to fight
My heart is heavy
My mind full of doubt
I pray and wait, wait and pray
Oh Lord, my Lord
Fight, fight, and fight this battle
The words I have hidden in my heart
They are not forming in my mouth
I cry during the day, I cry during the night
My love for you, I do not hide
Daily I try to thank you for all you have done for me
Please, oh please Lord
Fight, fight, and fight this battle
My armor is on from head to toe
Fight, fight, and fight this battle
Kid one is all grown up
Now working on kid two and three
Fight, fight, fight this battle
Trying to speak and teach your word
To the young and old
Sick and well
Head held high, head hung low
Fight, fight, and fight this battle
Almighty God, fight, fight, fight this battle

Joyce Hudson
Indianapolis, IN

Hello, my name is Joyce Hudson. I am a mother of three children and one grandchild. I enjoy reading and writing poems and short story. I graduated from Ivy Tech with an associate degree in human service. The poem "Fight This Battle" came about dealing with life issues. I had a revelation that I was not alone.

Feeling the Sun

Feeling the sun.
Warmth of light.
Higher as it rises,
Souring through the sky.
It takes its sweet time.
Feel the prime of its rays while both giving and receiving energy.
Yes my darling sun has the power to do both.
The sun brings both tears and joy.
A comparison of love, too much is toxic and to little is depressing.
We must be careful with our beautiful blessing.
The key is to stay humble.
We learn this from the sun.
Move like the sun, giving the world your perfect amount of light to thrive on.
So that we may all continue...
Feeling the sun.
Warmth of light.
Higher as it rises,
Souring through the sky.

Brianna Danae Treadway
Fontana, CA

I am a twenty-seven-year-old mother of a ten-year-old son from Los Angeles, CA. Poetry is a way for me to escape into my own spirituality. It allows me to disconnect from reality while still being attached. Poetry is a way for love to be disbursed on a high scale. The sun is fascinating to me and that is why I chose to include it in this piece that I am sharing with you. I absolutely hope you all melt while reading my poem. If not melt, then smile!

Fallen

A fall drive to the Virginia state line,
My mind goes back in time.
Seeing signs on the mountain wall,
A legend comes to call
About a young Indian maid
And how she lost her life.
She was out on a ledge, on a
Mountain trail.
As the story goes,
No one knows.
What happened on that dreadful day,
Lots of rumors, as they say.
She was to wed a young Indian brave,
But a love story came to an end that day.
We will never know what happened
Since the tragic loss
Of the girl known as fallen rock;
Her story leaves you in shock.
When the sun makes your eyes blink,
You'll recall and think:
Of the legend of Fallen Rock.

Wilma Lee Shifflett
Mt. Crawford, VA

My travels to West Virginia are what inspired me to write this poem. The signs on the mountain walls that say "fallen rock" reminds me of an Indian girl, so I attempted to write a poem about her. I had surgery recently and haven't felt my best, but I tried. I like to daydream about love stories. I'm a hopeless romantic. I've worked on this poem for a while since I haven't written a poem in a while ... lots going on in my life right now! Hope everyone enjoys my poem about fallen rock.

Drought

Happiness used to splash from your eyes
Soaking everyone around you
Your laughter lifted spirits
Making all laugh with yours
Your joy used to be what I fed off of
What brought me joy
Then one day everything changed
Something tore that toxic joy from your heart
That heart that used to swell with light
I tried to salvage any remains of happiness that dripped out of your eyes,
The little happiness that shed from your fading smile
The downpours became showers
The showers became drizzles
The drizzles became droplets
And soon enough those droplets will become droughts
I will never stop dreaming of the happiness that once leaked from your soul
And I'll never leave,
I'll wait,
I'll wait until you are replenished with those downpours that used to fill the streams that swelled your heart
Those streams that fill my ocean.

Olivia S. Kelsey
Tempe, AZ

Hello! My name is Olivia Kelsey and I actually published a smaller e-book when I was sixteen, five years ago. I'm a huge lover and empath in this world and I feel people's happiness, sadness, and everything in between. This poem is inspired by me feeling and— first and foremost—witnessing a loved one fall into a depression that I wanted to pull her out of, but in the end we all know only we can make our choices, no matter how much we may try to influence happiness on someone else. This poem is real, when one experiences sadness within another human being, while also having immense love for them as well.

Dear Mike

Many moons and many suns
have passed me by...
and yet, still, a memory of you is in my mind's eye.
So many thoughts of you, and how it could've been...
It's like a whirlwind; just makes my head spin!
Where are you, my forever love?
Years ago, we danced and danced and danced,
even when the music stopped.
The d.j. said, "looks like love on the dance floor!"
I thought you'd be my forevermore.
The sun rises and the sun sets
on this ancient heartache.
Then, night-time comes.
I look at the moon and I look at the stars.
It's then, I'm reminded, that destiny just wasn't ours.

Robin Lynne Melet
West Carrollton, OH

Once, when I was in college, I met a beautiful person named Mike. I love him to this day and am grateful I met him. He, sadly, is the one who got away. He was so nice to me. This is for all the "ones who got away." May we all find the healing in our hearts to love again.

Daddy's Gentle Smile

My first love, I knew no other
Always with a gentle smile
Daddy prayed with Mom each morning day.
Peeking through their bedroom door
Must have been three or four
Quietly I stood as Dad kissed Mom ending morning prayer each new day.
Tiptoe, tiptoe sliding through the wooden floors
Jumping back to bed with eyes closed
Waiting for the warmth of his gentle kiss upon my forehead
My heart rejoicing I was Daddy's special princess secured in all his love.
I could still see his face with saddened eyes.
He waved his hand to Mom with a gentle smile closing the door
My heart fluttered missing him as he left to work faithfully.
Faithfully returning home with a bag of treats
We jumped with joy in his embrace with the widest smile our daddy was home.
Mom proudly set the dinner table with Dad's special dishes fit for a king.
Closing our eyes we listened as he prayed the Lord's Prayer
Giving thanks for all we had
As Mom held our new baby brother in her arms
Dad joyfully reached to kiss his little hands every evening as we ate.
Faithfully you always remained wherever your footsteps led you in life
For four generations you remained I knew in my heart you was our gift from God
In love with you Daddy we always felt your love for us all.
Memories cherished and inscribed in the depths of our hearts
Never to be forgotten we live today
In memory of your sweet gentle smile.

Ipolita Sanchez
Brooklyn, NY

This poem I dedicate to Dad, Gregorio Sanchez Montalvo, born on March 10, 1931 in Mayaguez, PR. Thank you, Dad, for your faithfulness and the love you gave us all. Through it all you taught us that family is sacred and we must always pray and be there for one another no matter what life might bring. For love and compassion are the greatest gifts towards all of God's children. We thank God for you Dad and know that you went to be with Jesus on August 10, 2018, reigning in God's kingdom in eternal love. Your daughter, "Polita"—"Mi Molleta."

Bring Joy and Love To Others

Bring joy and love to others;
It's the order of the day.
It can be small, a hug or a smile,
Something that we do or say.

A deed of kindness can go a long way
To enabling someone to have an uplifting day.
To show that we care, what a difference it makes;
Always find something positive in others,
That's all that it takes!

In this current crazy world of ours
Hostility everywhere has created quite a mess.
So let's turn the tables around.
And concentrate on imparting happiness.

Music and humor unite people everywhere.
Our Lord created each of us;
We need to appreciate the "oneness" of us all.
Uniquely, He adores us. He watches over us from above.
So let's get our act and purpose together,
And to everyone we know and meet,
Let's bring joy and love.

Sharon Chazan
Boca Raton, FL

Sharon Ruth Chazan was born and raised in Montreal, Quebec, Canada. She received her bachelor of music degree from McGill University in Montreal and her masters in music theory and composition from the University of Miami. She was and continues to be inspired by the late Dora Wasserman of Blessed Memory, director of the Yiddish Theatre Drama Group in Montreal. Sharon started writing poetry at the age of nine.

BKFL Checks Out

Walks out, leaving your mind contorted and trapped in swath
of negativity charged charcoal clouds,
Your last words never quite made it out of your vocal cords,
Internal mental security is breached, now causing panic,
Similar to humans with sharks in the water developing into a fear of the beach,
Emotions running rampant,
Forcing your behavior into the beginning stages of lucid and manic,
And when they meet in the middle, you become sandwiched,
Also struggling desperately with your long since forgotten old best friends,
Lost and delirious again, although timeless and classic,
They come together wrapped in blurry plastic,
Another special edition two box set with Barbie and Ken,
The word SORRY always comes in packs of at least ten,
And after that many, you will stop digesting them, such a simple term
being spewed out of ones mouth covered in ageless layers of vocabulary
abuse by every woman and man,
All over this planet from West to East and North to South,
Next time try not to shout, be more understanding,
Compromising is a good foundational route,
Sitting down is key when talking to your lover and trying to solve
problems and work vicious cycles out, so cast away all the doubt and blame,
Fill in all the exposed crevices with truth and remain loyal and respectful,
Never call one another out of name,
Because dropping the first seed of hate can quickly slip right through the
guards rake traveling very fast down between the sharp green blades of grass,
Soon being watered with tears and nurtured with fears every day and
every night,
Fight after fight, that tree of life will grow so extremely quick and tall,
You can't handle it getting to a point where it grows out of sight,
Higher than a kite, only left in shaded beds of lies,
Definitely no sunshine on either side of the walls or fault lines that they
had to dig to have; this will ensure both of you are left empty and sad,
Stop inflicting mental anguish into every dimension of your brain just
because you're all mad.

Dean C. Grube
San Jacinto, CA
This was inspired by my soul twin and the struggle thru life and all its perils remaining together no matter what and finding a way if at times impossible to work problems out. Infinity M.B.

Viking Warfare

I left my home, the world to roam
it's been now twelve years gone.
From a boy to a man
was a dreadful short span,
as I journeyed to valleys beyond.
Now the king, he has spoken
and battle has broken,
I'm wise to the ways of the world.
Long on the sword,
as we seek our reward,
to see our flag unfurled…
Sailed by starry dark of night,
our longships cross the sea.
Where a hundred headless horsemen
guard the gates of Galilee.
Each dawn's a daily dance of death,
 through battle smoke like dragon's breath.
With echo axe to armor chink,
each onslaught we rebuffed.
You can invite the devil for a drink
 …if you think you're man enough.
Heavy's the head that wears the crown,
when the blood of brothers' beckons.
Weak is the sword, as it lies on the ground.
If there's a will, there's a way,
there are weapons.
But once the battle has ended
and our journeys' been made,
there'll be air in my lungs,
and blood on my blade.

Cole Banner
Melissa, TX

Battles

Do you ever feel ready to face your demons head on
Like you have enough strength to overcome anything?
Maybe it's a certain song
Or a thought that comes in the quiet after a battle,
And you go out with the confidence of an army.
And then that next battle comes
And you fall.
It was a small one, a mere poke with a stick,
And yet you went down like a tree to an axe.
Because it's not the visible enemy you're fighting,
No matter how big or small.
Behind every unique battle is the same demon,
The demon of understanding—or lack thereof.
You fear it will destroy the world you hold together
The minute you turn your back.
When you, your own savior, feel like you're crumbling,
It's hard to trust anything, especially yourself.
And that leaves me trapped in my own mind,
Drowning in the ocean of anxiety I created,
Barely keeping my head above water—
But above all, too ashamed to cry for help.

Victoria Elise Deaton
Saint Petersburg, FL

My name is Victoria, I'm nineteen, and I'm a preschool teacher. While trying to think of a topic to write about for this competition, I thought of this poem, one I'd written about my anxiety after a particularly rough bout. I decided to use it, because I think it expresses my personal anxiety and how it affects me in an interesting light. The end of the poem touches on my inability to talk about my struggles. Maybe someone can relate to this, maybe not. It's just a little glimpse into my mind. One day I'll be free—I'm believing it.

As a Child

Lord Jesus, as a child I come to You
As one who sees Your world so fresh and new,
As one who finds delight in simple things,
Who almost hears the song creation sings.
As one who sees all nature sparkled bright,
As one who runs and plays with sheer delight,
As one who trods life's gardened path secure,
For in Your love, I'm safe forevermore.
Filled with sense of wondered, pure delight,
Awed to see the star-filled joys of night,
Amidst sun-sparkled beauty as I play,
Enjoy this dazzled world that You have made.
    And love You, Lord, in ways both sweet and wild
    Completely as a joy-filled, wondered child.

Joyce Keedy
Towson, MD

As a music teacher, I have taught nearly nine hundred children and adults to play musical instruments. An organist of one church for twenty-nine years, I am now an organist/choir director of another church since 2016. And always to the glory of God! Lord Jesus is my strength, my song, my matchless Lord and Savior, and my eternal joy. One of the many gifts He has given me is that of retaining the same fresh sense of joy and wonder I knew as a child. This poem will be included in my ninth book of poems to be published in early 2020.

Arigato Mary (Thank You, Mary)

When I was a little girl, Mary planted a seed of faith in me.
She came one Sunday and took me to her Japanese Christian church.
Mama did not say no, so I went to Mary's church.
My Buddhist parents then made Sunday beach fun day.
Now . . . no one is home. For we are at the beach.
Then as a young woman living in Hawaii, my life changed.
A handsome "hakujin" (caucasian) marine came into my life.
After Vietnam, he went off to Frisco; his goal was to be a music man.
Four years I waited, then I said, "Don't come again to see me."
Then he called back and said, "Let's get married."
He came down to LA to get me, and off to Vegas we went.
This marriage, with Mama, not okay. Seems she was right.
Seven years go by and his PTSD healed.
Then off he went with someone else.
Going home on the mountain road came a whisper, "turn that wheel."
God gave me strength to say no to the devil. My boys, my reason
to live and not commit suicide.
My husband had said to abort the baby. If I had I would now be dead.
Planted so long ago, that faith seed began to grow.
That faith seed into full bloom it burst; a comfort to me.
My six year old got chicken pox and then the baby got it, too.
I prayed to God at the hospital, and God healed my baby.
My Earth angel Mary now lives in Bakersfield with her family.
A two-hour drive, three times a year church members visit Mary.
Thank you, God, for the seed she planted so long ago.
And so, I'm still alive today.

Michiko Tokunaga Kus
San Fernando, CA

Shigeko from Mary's prior church invites me to their "Super Senior Luncheons." A thank you, she said, for cheering up her hubby Ken with his favorite cowboy story books. These I got from Chuck and Charla Pereau who, fifty plus years ago, started a mission to Mexico called Foundation for His Ministry. Shigeko's husband is now home in Heaven as promised in John 3:16. A pastor shared, if you get a nudge to do something and it's not mean, it's probably a nudge from God. Those two kind ladies get that nudge, and zip, they do it.

An Unmentioned Lifestyle

It is wonderful oh so wonderful to have
The love, support, kindness, and moral compassion
Of a wonderful and outstanding mother and father
When one unfortunately leads
An unmentioned lifestyle
The lifestyle of sickle-cell disease
It's so saddening others on this planet
It's oh so saddening no one else seems to care
Which for some reason I can't understand
For some reason concern they just don't share
It's not like it's an illness of every race
Or at least that's what the majority wants you to believe
Or maybe it's something else going on with
Since nowadays everyone practices to deceive
Physicians, nurse practitioners chiefly in ER's and pain management
Who are supposed to help you especially with your pain?
Act like you are a liar or a redundant nuisance
In September, National Sickle-Cell Month
Nobody wishes to nationally stand up to sickle-cell
And even the ones who interact with a victim often and rather well
Question constantly that it can't be that bad or they have it made
Unfortunately that is not true at all
Restrictions in life is another item I must tell
A large cross one must bear which no one can understand
An unmentioned lifestyle isn't grand

Julius Collins
Norris, SC

I am just a human being with a terminal recessive genetic disorder. It is sickle-cell anemia. It has restricted my life and has caused me many a day of pain and hospitalization. My doctors have used me as a guinea pig many a day. I was denied a bone marrow transplant at seventeen, so the illness just worsens. They said I wouldn't live past seventeen, but I have. I write short stories. I write poetry and songs. I am a didactic. I have also majored in industrial electronics technology. I am a freelance photographer. God has been my strength as well as my parents. I am also a musician and have been told I can sing many a song.

An Immigrant

For long I had searched for safety
Red stripes and white, fifty stars on blue waving in the wind
A symbol of freedom for me
A permit to put behind
Years of horror and fear

What if my family is separated?
My parents manipulated and abused,
My child put in a cage, washed to shore
or mentally confused?
What if an evil plot makes those closest to me turn their head around

I hear, "Come in, here is the place of your dreams"
But my dream deferred
It's long my parents are gone
My siblings are foes, my children diverted from their goal
What-ifs turned true

Horror of bomb no longer of foe
It's the covert neighbor next door
Fear of gun is from the protector
Afraid of being shot, shoots the child
Playing with a toy gun in the yard

Mitra Pourmehr
San Rafael, CA

In 1980 when war broke out between Iran and Iraq my children were one and four years old. Daily bombardments and fear of the children being left in the rubbles hungry and cold made me stitch my sister's telephone number on my little boy's clothes and my daughter memorized the number. When my sister heard, she applied for me and my family. We expected a two-year waiting period, which was extended to seventeen years. At the time I was summoned, my daughter had passed twenty-one and was no longer eligible to enter the United States, and my son who was eighteen was not able to leave Iran for military service there.

A Year in December

He was dying in slow motion.
There was nothing I could do.
And cancer is like a fire,
and once it spreads, you're doomed.
His hand was hers to hold
until that December night.
But Christmas is just like any day,
and it can't save a life.
The lights on the tree danced,
but I never dreamed they'd burn out.
And the most wonderful time of year,
felt like a nightmare in this house.
It'll be a year in December,
but I can remember the way your laugh sounds.
And every November, I still remember
hunting was all you wanted to talk about.
And every October, I would come over,
and we'd decorate for Halloween.
But it'll be a year in December
since cancer took you away from me.
It was like someone opened a door,
and let the cold air fill my room.
I begged God not to take him,
but I didn't want anyone else in my shoes.
And Nana had to learn how to love again,
but she's still not at peace.
And every October, you would come over,
and you'd sing Happy Birthday to me.
It'll be 14 years in December,
but it still feels like yesterday to me.

Shayla Mayhugh
Chickasha, OK

A Love Poem

Love is never harsh or hard as metal
but is gentle and kind and soft as a rose petal.
Love is a word you love to find
in a note, in a letter, or a card that's been signed.
Love is in a marriage when a couple are wed.
Love is in their hearts as the vows are said.
But to keep love alive it has to be fed
by caring and sharing in words that are said.
And actions more precious than words can convey
true feelings of love each and every day.
There's more happiness in giving than receiving.
If surely it is true because I'm giving and sharing
this love poem with you.

Virginia Sanders
Chapmanville, WV

I was married for fifty-three and a half years until my husband passed away with bone cancer. I believe observing commands and principles in God's word. The Bible is the key to a happy family life.

343

Once the first strike hit-it was like dominoes falling.
The 343 unlike you and me faced their deaths without a second thought.
Selflessly, they lived in hell their last moments;
but gained wings to fly home in the end where the angels sing.
Evil had planned to hurt the world that particular day—
to destroy lives—to kill as many innocent people that got in its way.
Fueled by hate, it waited patiently, lurking amongst those it despised so.
Once the alarms sounded, the 343 donned their gear and set out to the unknown hell that awaited them.
They entered the gates of flames to this hell, putting their lives on the line to never exit again.
These brothers were bound by bond stronger than blood.
Their motto in life was "You go! We go!"
The question has long been asked, "For Whom the Bell Tolls?"
You see, it tolled for the 343...calling home their souls that fateful day.
Blessed be-the mighty-the brave-the fallen 343. May their sacrifice never be forgotten.

Shannon L. O'Kelley
Gordo, AL

This poem was inspired by 9/11. I'm a former firefighter/first responder. This is dedicated to the my brothers and sisters. May their sacrifices never be forgotten.

Your World and Mine

You were once in my world; you made me smile, held me
close, gave me a special part of your life. You touched
me with your sweet words and loving smile. Now the
world that was once ours has crumbled and fell.

The room that was filled with laughter is filled with tears.
The guitar that was filled with music sits silent and still.
A world that we may someday know is yet to be ours in God's
heavenly home where you will be able to play your music.

You reached out with music in your walk here on Earth.
There were so many things planned that you wanted to do.
God saw you weaken and whispered, Mark, come with Me
to God's heavenly home where you can play your drums.

Up in Heaven there will be a home of entire beauty with
much love and happiness. When we shall meet I will know
what your world was like—a life filled with love and music.
This will be your home; that will be mine. Forever, Korena.

Helen Wilson
W. Alexander, PA

This poem was written in memory of our son Robert Mark. He was sixteen when he died and was a member of the band at McGuffey High School. Upon his death the school set up a scholarship and spirit award in his name. Each year two worthy members of the senior band are presented these awards.

Vincent's Starry Night Eclipses

Crows over wheat field
Invaders of golden field,
Black blotches of crows, be gone!
Black winding sheet,
Hovering over Vincent's soul,
Lethal chaperones, leave his mind alone!
Swoop out of your museum frame,
Ride the universal love waves
Glowing in Vincent's "Starry Night"
Peck on its whirling dervish brush strokes,
Your black hearts will swirl to mystical heights.
See glittering ovaries streaming
Through the fallopian milky blue.
As two mammoth waves embrace,
Gaze in awe at the cervix formed
For cosmic entry by the moon,
Shush your caws during union in night skies.
The town snuggles like a child In the rolling hills
As cypress flames rise . . .
Black fiends, marauding golden fields,
Like thoughts gnawing at Vincent's sanity.
Know this "Starry Night's" illuminations
Will always eclipse your evil augury!

Lily Georgick
Jackson Heights, NY

I believe Vincent experienced great inner joy and peace that he expressed in this masterful, mystical painting.

Recollections

Memories last a long while
Recalling brings a warm smile
With its happiness is simply simple
At time life becomes silent
Engraving thoughts your style
Embodies smiles in the heart
Sincerity it's all it takes
Memories can't be replaced by emptiness

A warm smile covers the wounds
Living in a world that's cold
Life span is growing gradually short
Stress runs like running water
Memories at times gives us comfort
We are humans with a smile our shelter
In life you have a beautiful soul
In life in this world you have a role

Memories and journey are like coffee
You taste & create your own flavor
Sit back sip on your cup of tea
Memories at the end is what you savor!

For the person yearning inside
Good and bad I'll stand by your side
For every smile you only give
And receive another day to live
The greatest thing to achieve
Warm memories the soul alone
Memories keeps us alive
A place we feel safe and call home.

Claudia Walthing
Hanford, CA

After a major event in my life after an eight-hour brain surgery when I died for a moment lead me to see poetry in motion. I appreciate every little and big thing in this journey called life here on Earth. Share love with the world with a good deed or smiles to those you meet through your life. Don't forget you are here for a reason not just because, so make the best of life. I am thankful to wake up every day and with a smile to share.

My Legendary Halterman Stepdad

In my mind he was a legend in his own time. At eight years old he had polio (In a photo he wore bibbed overalls and stood cute by his bearded dad who was tall and died in a coal mine I was told.). He and Mom married when I was about fourteen months old. They had a good start but sad troubles and work problems began to sprout. History of our main neighborhood where he grew up had been called "The Western Front." Maybe John Wayne should have been his given name. He could be hilarious, yet tough times made him madly insane! I, as his stepchild, loved his mother very much. She was a sweet elderly widow who lived alone. At times we'd all go to church—he even helped drive a church bus. Again, tougher times came around. We eventually moved from near his mother to Mom's former hometown. He liked TV westerns and such. His geology in life had that similar touch. Mom divorced him after several hard years. After he passed, a few of us still spoke of him at times. I trust God all found peace and forgiveness at last, for we've all had a legendary past.

Frances Elaine Camp
Americus, GA

Before school age I was "sometimes" proud I had three daddies—my real dad, my stepdad (who became an alcoholic), and my grandfather who was nicknamed Daddy Bill to us kids. The movie I Can Only Imagine was a touch to my life as a stepchild at times. I left home at age fourteen to care for an invalid, elderly great-great-aunt in 1961. In past years, I was on a chair volleyball team with other senior citizens in Wellston, OH and attended county bingo one year. I helped steer a stern wheeler boat on the Ohio River. I flew on five airplane flights in 1970.

Echoes of Childhood

Share-croppers were we when I was a lad.
Very little money we had.
Even five cents as measly a fare, for a
lowly ice cream cone, for us was a
hard token to bear.
We roamed from farm to farm, until
1951, when at last we settled in the old
"Bryson Hollow," in the Cannon County hills
of Aburn Tennessee.
Happy were we there till 1954, when
February 11th, mighty flames did roar.
My mother and children three, barely escaped
that fatal and cruel day, when everything
we loved was taken away.
No time to take any belongings, great or
small, for some sixty seconds later
our roof did fall.
Yes, echoes of this still peal.
For me, it is still too real.
For psychological scars in all disdain
forever still remain.

Vernon Bogle
Manchester, TN

Vision of Temptation

Outside the window
I see lights that glow;
Cars park everywhere
In the kitchen over there.

Caught up in a crowd
That is so loud,
Lost in the midst of food
That tastes really good.

Drift on the lovely music
Everyone looks chic;
Amazing beauty
It's like eternity.

Eyes are dreary
Body that sway,
Walk like a snake
Stumble like a cake.

Inside the point of view
Is a silent adieu;
The music stops
As I begin to flop.

Maricel Hardel
Phoenix, AZ

Again and Again

I miss you so much
I can't believe the fears
In your eyes
How are you doing
How have you been

When the finger of change
When the past will it
comes around
What are you thinking
What are you doing

Then it's all over here
Then it's all starting
Again and Again
Can we be together
Can we make a new start

I miss you so much
I can't believe the tears
in your eyes
How are you doing
How will you be

James Fred Brinkman
Bismarck, ND

Untitled

what am I
a shadow
a mere speck in the spectrum of space and time
so then, how can my heart be so full
yet my life so dull—my mind so loud
while my voice vanishes in the crowd
why do I feel so deeply and sense so much
if only I could touch my destiny
without the necessity to think in crashing waves
in a blink we're gone
what I crave, to move on
I'm walking a straight line to the valleys
of remembrance
do not be fooled by a broken,
a damaged heart that shows repentance
a matter of time to change the semblance
a matter of time to give a sentence
It's a game
a maze in the sky of the human brain
give a name
there's nothing else to do but for history to refrain
pick a side
it won't matter as the years come by
look at you
answer my question in a second or two
What are you

Oriana Morales
Hialeah, FL

A little over four years ago, I arrived to the United States from Venezuela, my country of birth, at eleven years old. I had to face the uncertainty of entering a new culture, new people, and new experiences. I began writing as a way to channel the suffering of my daily life, emerging with my inability to cope with my parents' failing marriage and the language barrier. This poem came as a response to an existential question, for I was questioning my purpose as a whole—just like everyone else, one minuscule universe of atoms against the world.

Angels Below the Sky

I'm an angel flying high above the sky,
Looking down at his creation called mankind.
Their selfish behaviors bring tears to my eyes.
How can they stand and watch from the sidelines,
As their brothers and sisters struggle to survive?

It appears their hearts have hardened,
like stones by the riverside.
I pray they behold the beauty they carry on the inside.
But as these thoughts play, reel to reel in my mind!
I slowly open my eyes and to my surprise, I realized.
We are all angels below the sky.

Dane L. Robinson
Bronx, NY

My name is Dane Robinson, and I am a poet from New York City. I developed the love for poetry at the age of twelve, but I didn't start writing until the age of fifteen. The inspiration for this poem came to me from observation. The way we treat each other demonstrates a lack of compassion for our fellow humans. We would do anything to get our own way; everything is about self, instead of "we." I believe if we unite and work as one we will get a lot more accomplished. A bird cannot fly without the help of its wings and the wind of the sky.

Seasonal Depression

I find myself untangling headphones
With frozen fingers. I was not made for
The cold winter. Seasonal Depression
Is just depression under feet of snow.
My brain has been buried beneath blizzards,
My heart craves the sun. I don't ever give
Myself enough time to think. But things are
Finally getting better, I think. My
Therapist tells me I'm doing okay,
But she doesn't know, there are so many

Insecurities and demons knocking.
They push at the doors of my heart, whining.
But, I've found, as each day passes, there is
One fewer insecurity prying.

Julia Rose Casale
Boxford, MA

This poem was inspired by wandering around my university campus on a snow day, feeling kind of hollow and bored. It was sonnet-inspired, with fourteen lines, ten syllables each, and a tone shift in the last two lines. I still find it relevant in other seasons, where depression has permeated through the weather and follows you around all year.

Love Is Not Singular

Love is not singular; it is plural.
It has many forms and can multiply
When it is given freely—unconditionally.

Love is not jealous; it is giving and empathetic
To all those who find it and can erase all hate
When it's loving and kind without malice or envy.

Love is not easy; it is difficult at times.
It takes all the wisdom and energy you can gather.
When it's right in front of you, it takes a lot of soul-searching.

Love is not guilty; it is innocent.
It engulfs your heart and soul and mind
With acceptance and appreciation and affection
And fills you up with life-sustaining nectar.

Love is not anything; it is everything!
it gives you the power and wisdom to overcome all obstacles
And finds truth to be the answers to all your questions.

Love is not singular . . . love everyone!

Donna M. Mitchell
Kingston, PA

11 Years

11 years of laughter.
11 years of tears.
11 years of fun times.
11 years of fears.
11 years remembered and many more to go.
11 years have come and gone.
11 years ago.
11 years of firsts... the first to hold my hand and hear my beating heart.
11 years and I've loved you from the start.
11 years have come and gone.
11 years and I'm the one who gets to be your mom.
11 years of wondering if I've done it right.
11 years of "just winging it" at times.
11 years I can't believe it. I wish the days would slow.
11 years how can it be, where did the time go?

Amber Sue Reinhart
Orefield, PA

When My Time Has Come

When my time has come,
The bells will ring,
The birds will sing,
The butterflies will flutter.
A glorious sight
The angels sing;
The night sky will be bright;
The stars and moon
Will twinkle with glee;
For another angel has come to he.
So don't cry for me,
I'm in a better place you see.
Be joyful

Sheila Evans
Forest City, NC

Remain True

What to do
To remain true
To who you are
So you don't stray far

Know what your truths are
Don't let outside pressure or opposition
Set you ajar
Stick to your beliefs core
And you will be pure
And be who you are
No matter the lumps and bumps
You might endure
No matter the scars.

Bernadette Bonacci
Philadelphia, PA

From This Point On . . .

From this point on I wanna have some say I wanna hear my voice when I exercise my rights in my power of choice and not listen to those voices that have me making those choices that leave me with regret, heartache, and shame and have me dragging through the mud my oh so precious name. From this point on, I want to change my views and change my reactions. When I get bad news so come what may, come what will it's out of my control, it's all God's will so let me stop fighting with what is and what was. It is what it is, and it was what it was that being said I see things clearer and get down to business with the man in this mirror. It is with self that I have the biggest fight so let me fight the good fight from this point on. From this point on I want to have my own because God bless the child that has his own but he still shows grace to the ones who have not and the ones who do dirt to get what they got, but this ain't about they, this is all about me doing all I can to be all I can be, to use what I have to get what I need. God dwells within so why should I go without from this point on? From this point on, Lord, I pray to do Your will each and every day and what is your will? Heaven only knows but I pray for revelation as time goes I pray that it shows and then I'll know and then I'll grow and then I can go and let everybody know that I've tasted grace, that I'm still in the race, and when it's all said and done I want to see God's face in all Its glory sitting on His throne thy will be done from this point on.

Nelson F. Young
Pembroke Pines, FL

I'm forty-six years old and I know a lot about starting over; I've done it so many times. I've made a lot of mistakes and a lot of bad decisions. I've lost a lot of friends, relationships, and material possessions but more importantly I've lost a lot of spiritual battles. Ironically, it has been through the process of losing that I've had my greatest victories. They have made me the man I am today. Sure, the maturation process has taken longer than normal (but what is normal?), but I can honestly say that I have no regrets. Sure, there are things that I wish I could have done differently, but I have no regrets. Today I have a full life and I have a great life! I am so very grateful for all the failures, the trials, and the tribulations and shortcomings. Writing has always been an outlet for me, and I hope that things I've been through will inspire someone else to not make the same mistakes. Life is good. Please enjoy it while it lasts.

Old in Logan

Grey hair,
wrinkled skin,
knobby joints,
wobbling gait—
you've passed your prime,
a testament of advancing age.
You've exchanged your tiny grocery—your brainchild
for the government handout,
for the social security check that was stolen
as you boarded a noonday bus.
You've chosen fear.
Golden padlocks glisten on your front door,
sunlight streams diffused through grated windows.
Your cane becomes the beating stick
for muggers possessing twice your sinews,
for burglars with pistols.
You've become the prisoner
forsaking your youth,
growing old in Logan.

Lynette Bajsarowycz
Philadelphia, PA

Ink of My Blood

I scribble in a translation
Of my inner language
Through a dagger
The length of my fluent hand
Flickering, flitting
Along my arched fingers
It is compressed in lines as smooth,
Articulate as the pin prick of ink
Free flowing through cursive waves
Curving the ink of my blood
Out in the open it spills
In a display of viscera
The insides of my chest cavity
Spewing contents of what are
My inner-most thoughts
Dreams, vulnerabilities, aspirations
Translating through my rambling language
From that single dagger
Flickering, flitting
Like a free verse butterfly
Dripping the ink of my blood
From paper thin wings

Chrissy Bortz
Latrobe, PA

I'm Grandma

As I get older
I have slowed down my pace.
Unfortunately I get in trouble
for expressions on my face.
Now I grunt and groan
while trying not to speak.
I laugh underneath my breath.
I constantly move my feet.
My kids and grandkids
think sometimes that I am a pain.
Remember I like singing out loud.
I love dancing in the rain.
I would softly kiss you
on your little noses.
I'm a teacher and a nurse.
I'm grandma; I wiggle little toes.
I will always love you.
I know you all love me.
I will always be proud.
You are all my family.

Debra Tovatt
Palm Harbor, FL

Our Brother Bill

Our time together has come and gone;
where did it go? We always thought we would go on and on.
You were the leader, always getting us through the ups and downs.
"Come on, let's go, no time to mess around."

You always wanted to be early, never late;
it was important to you not to make people wait.
Fishing was a big part of your life;
it calmed you and made you forget the strife.

When you caught the "big one" there was no stopping
your big grin and sparkling green eyes.
You would say, "Are you watching your bobber?
You need to bring in a big one! Come on, you guys."

You watched and talked sports all the time;
you loved to tease us about our teams,
saying they're never going to win—
it's just a dream.

We think about you every day,
believing you will still always lead the way.
Although we shall see you no more, as we must accept God's will,
you will forever be, our brother Bill.

Trish Ellen Weidner
Hanover Township, PA

A Blur

Think I scored a lucky strike,
my miserable stars finally aligned
and I'll never forget.
I'll always remember how we first met.
My body froze as my lips trembled;
I hated what I resembled.
My insides wrecked with anxiety;
I never thought I'd regain my sanity.
I rushed to the nearest table.
As I slowly tried to get stable
my eyes wandered around, but it was all a smudge.
It was all until I felt a little nudge.
I peeled my eyes away from the crowd
and set them on someone who wasn't as loud.
She had a warm smile and short dark hair;
I had never seen a beauty like her there.
"I like your sweater," she whispered;
her voice alone made me blush.
"Thanks," I muttered, looking at anything but her.
Maybe this was more than a girl crush.
My vision finally cleared itself from the constant blur.
I wondered if my heart was mistaken
But maybe it was time it'll finally awaken.
I was pretty young when this took place
But it'll take me ages to ever forget her face.

Tanvi Kumar
Monmouth Junction, NJ

I'm Tanvi C. Kumar, a junior at SBHS. A while ago, I was assigned a "contrast poetry" project in English. I brainstormed ideas for ages till I settled on one. I decided to write about the first time I realized I wasn't straight. I was raised in New Delhi where LGBT was taboo. This poem is based on a very vivid memory I had of meeting Susan, a girl who made me realize liking her wasn't so odd after all. "A Blur" refers to how tons of queer kids—like me—look at their lives before coming out.

Love Torture

I wonder why we do this
Love and care to venom so abusive
Is this really conducive
Seems so ludicrous
Take someone's heart to misuse it
Is love really this elusive
Nothing is more bold
Than to let someone see into your soul
Speak aloud what your heart has told
Two hearts and lives bend and fold
Begin to mend and end in a new mold
Even more precious than gold
But oh how deep the lows will go
Scars cut past flesh and bone
Shredding your heart and soul
More pain than anyone should know
What warms your heart with life's glow
Will freeze it, leave it frostbitten like snow
Buried in woe 6 feet below
We fight the ones we love
No rules, no gloves
But shouldn't lovers be above
Malice and spite and vengeful acts
Painfully sad and dreadful facts
Maybe you pay the price in fact
For shooting lead full dice in craps
But still my question remains
Is this really love or pain
Or are they one in the same

Milagros Dominic Ray Rizo
Greeley, CO

Heavenly Angel

O heavenly angel sitting high above,
perfecting and guiding your flock
as they travel across the land.

As time and days pass from light to dark
you illuminate the sky with twinkling stars
that brighten for miles.

O heavenly angel
thank you for each day and night,
for we are guided.

Without you we will be lost!

Dee Gushea
Bellmawr, NJ

Words

I struggle to put
the thoughts of my mind
down on paper.
I continue to yearn
words from my soul into
thoughts of living.
I go to my quiet place
to meditate or assimilate
words of life into
thought that express my soul.
Can words coming from
within me be a substitute
for the writeen word of life?
Would one sell their soul
thus being able to take in
the unspoken living or
breath affirmations
to understood life.

Vickie Hannawell
Beloit, WI

Heated Lenses

I rested on a grassy hill—complete with a bed of roses,
and nestled underneath I willed
some rabbits' feet and noses!

I heard the bubbling of a brook so I took myself down to see,
as birds with a chuckling sound then looked,
boding well, frowning company . . .

With arms stretched out, I settled back to face a smile of blue,
(its charming guest had meddled and replaced my style of view).
The last of wine proved me aligned to bask in the fold of 3 senses.

'Ole Glory' this time moved that fury of mine
to a glass that controlled heated lenses!

Penelope H. White
New Kensington, PA

Whimsical, I wrote this thinking about kids in cages, or other things such as shootings, etc. The stuff of current America! This is about kids crying for family members. It hurt my heart (and heated up my eye glasses!).

but, words can never...?

Shadows gather;
The loud beating of my heart
Stops the roaring in my ears.
I did not seek this battle of bitter words
That pierce my heart like poisoned darts.
I wrap my bruised feelings
Around my wounded soul
And withdraw to the painful darkness
Of confusion.
The wound is deep,
The pain excruciating.

Betty Paschall Grantham
Goldsboro, NC

The Doctor Said

The doctor said,
"You have breast cancer."
What did he say?
What did I hear?
He said it again—
"You have breast cancer."
My mind filled with fear.
My husband! My children!
My life! Oh, so dear!
In one fleeting moment,
My mind filled with fear.
Then, my mind stopped
Long enough to say,
"You know God is in control
And he's here with you today
And he'll be with you tomorrow
To guide you, come what may."
I said, "Doctor,
I'm not afraid."

Pat Gregg
Oakland, IA

He Drew Himself

He drew himself in to a picture
Around his leg he wore a chain
He walked the desert sands
Until he was no longer the same

His pencil was sharpest at the beginning
Before his journey took its turn
He walked and walked without a word
Until the weight of the chain did burn

He wrote himself into a poem
No words could explain his distress
The pencil became the crutch he used
While he was writing his very best

The crutch became his tool
No one could ever understand
Why this man chose to cut off his foot
When it was there to help him stand

He wrote himself out of a prison
A place where life could not grow
He drew himself into the desert sands
Why he drew the sun so hot...
No one will ever know

Jennifer M. Shaw
Nashville, TN

The smell of fresh ink as the pen glides across my note pad, inventing something that no one else can call their own. Pouring out my heart into compassionate words, phrases, sentences brings the author, the writer, the poet in me alive. Remembering me means you saw my face or a likeness of me; however, remembering my words means I will live on . . . .

I Am a United States Veteran

I left home at eighteen
To fight in lands you've never seen
Except for on the tv screen
Baby killer some of you cry
You didn't have to choose to live or die
You spit on us and call us cowards
When we die you'll bring no flowers
You show up and protest our fight
After all it is your right
I did what I did for this great land
Now you come by and spit where I stand
I went where I must for Uncle Sam
To protect those I love in this great land
For you I put my life on the line
Now the VA can't see me in time
Tho my time of service has come to an end
I'll still defend this country to my very end
I am a United States veteran

Adrian J. Lovenduski
Troy, PA

Dark Forever Light

My cold midnight rain forest walk found glow worms.
Clinging to damp earth banks invisible by day
their shy phosphorescent pinpoints
glow delicate in forest night.

Vulnerable. Tiny. Flashlights frighten them closed.
Only darkness shows their reticent humble light.

Then in the clearing, above the branches.
What milky sheen is spilt upon the sky?

My shy eye can see such beauty only in darkness.
Web on web, light upon layer of reticent pinpoint light.

Stars are true, always with us
though only revealed in darkness.
Their reticence clarifies this tension with overwhelming day.
Our preposterous star claims too much of our time
overwhelming their true nature.

Steadfast, invisible except to the shy eye of darkness,
they accompany our each and every journey
surround our every moment.
Like ancient grandparents cheering,
they watch from afar.

Mary Rebecca Huie-Jolly
Jonesboro, GA

While a visitor to a remote part of the South Island of New Zealand, I wrote this poem in awe of humble light within the forest and the darkness of the night sky.

Wings of Dusk

What is the sky?
The sky is homeward bound
The sky has man
Blue as the eyes as one God-Man
In its hues we look and the sky is here
to the skyward when it leaves
A longing to life's treasures
A lighting of our needs come forward
But never to occur unkindly
Only to happen when it's raining
Is that the only time the thunder happens or occurs?

Nina Goldworth
Woodside, NY

I am honored to be one of the editors of Free Focus/Ostentatious Mind. Unfortunately my co-editor and the owner Patricia Denise Coscia passed away on August 29. 2019. I an interested in presenting her work and other poets and as an originator of the English language and a poetry devotee to teach children through my application. She was very inspirational to me and I am going to dedicate the book to her memory and our poetry entitled Poems for the Free Spirit. POSKISNOLT PRESS. *Included are about twenty-seven poets and some artists from my stomping grounds. "Wings of Dusk" is connected to my song "Homeward Bound" on the Simon & Garfunkel album* Sounds of Silence.

The Coal Miners

The miners work in the mines, so dark and damp
On their head a carbine lamp
They worked all day
To dig the coal away
A sturdy pick was their main tool
Sometimes they brought the coal out by mule
Man used to walk the mule on the railroad track
Their backs were bent from working in a small space
A canary to warn off air so foul, declaring dangerous air

Elizabeth Thompson
Blandburg, PA

The Beginning of Life

Now it starts, man is born of woman, just like you and me
You will soon find, that all of this will not be so free
When they hold by the legs and feet and slap your tender ass
This will start to pay for nine months ride of the passed
Then you can't walk or crawl, you can't do anything at all
But what I can do is lay there on your back and bawl
You will see I'll get even with them, I'll dirty my overalls
What! No stake and beans, all I get is this milky kind of stuff
Now if this was your kind of fare you'd call it, really rough
Wait till I get old enough to shop, I won't buy any of this slop
I'll just have ice-cream, cake and maybe a case of pop
Because this kind of treatment has got to stop
I'll make them pay one day

Martin P. McGarvey
Groveland, FL

Young Old Woman

To be worthy of peace, sampling imaginary perfection
These quandaries are answered in her form

I eye the land lost in her coat, a land of fox or mink
the collar upturned, the mountains,
covering the sunset that is painted on her lips

harshly attractive, her eyes pierce through the snow
blue flares absorbed in some secret I'll never know

lilacs bloom in her nostrils
warming the frigid air upon entry
she whispers softly through the stuffy night
the golden haze that baffled my ears

Fruits on wrinkled branches sprout from her brow
the apple tree - forbidden, I would die for a taste
she is the kind of star that leaves her lovers wrinkled
and yet still not a blemish on her face

Lovely folly in the crowd
The streets teem around her, but vacant are her eyes
a halo on her head; the fused wands of witches dead
She exists between the outside and an empty interior

Then she was gone.

Katherine Kallas
Shawnee, KS

Wind Chimes of Life

Wind Chimes of Life
Wind chimes twisting and turning in the wind,
Are like the twists and turns of life from beginning to end.
Weathered and worn the knots become frayed,
Taking the delightful sound away.

If bound by a chain will keep its strength for many years,
And the beautiful music we continue to hear.
But if rope or string, becoming weathered and worn,
The knots fray, then the beautiful sound becomes forlorn.

Just like life, as the years go by,
A heart grows stronger with tender care.
But if life brings heartache and lies,
The heart becomes broken and will tear.

Can the Wind Chimes be mended?
Will the twinkling sound no longer to hear,
Or, a broken heart be tended?
Do the gestures come from unknown fears?

Remembering back to another time, when I was sitting by the sea,
At the ending of another day when I was just a teen,
A sadness coming over me, even though it had been a wondrous time,
Foreshadowing my life of twists and turns -
The dawn of each day brings,
Influencing the changes occurring in your life and mine.

Denise E. Bowlin
Shreveport, LA

I am a country girl living in a big city wanting to return to a simple life. The poem was inspired by reflecting on events that have occurred in my life over the last few years. Life should be about God, family, and true friends.

Why?

Heavy double doors
    Enhanced with multicolored stained glass
        Maitre d' escorts us to our table
Menu reveals an array of choices
    Dinner—delicious cuisine
        Desserts—elegant, entwined with lemon zest.
           A second cup of coffee

"May I have the check?"

    "There is no check."
"What?"

"Why?"

    "It has been paid, madame."

"But, who?"

I searched the crowd for a clue.
    Perhaps, that person exiting the glass doors?

How do I say "Thank you?"

Someone whispered,
"Pay forward"

The heavy double doors are open.
    Tomorrow
        "Please be my guest."

Marilyn Peterson
Cozad, NE

Why Are You, You?

I was born a homosapien and I
never thought to ask the question, Why?
I was born and accepted being a man;
could I have been perhaps a dog or a toucan?
Why am I not a rabbit, snake, or bat—
perhaps a buffalo, a deer, or even a rat?

Preposterous most people will probably say
if they ever read this poem someday.
Of course we are who we are and there's no way
we could be anything or anyone else . . . okay!
But someday look your dog in the eye
and realize maybe he, too, is asking, why?

Think of all the people on this earth—
their colors, their looks, all coming at birth.
Think of their places in society
and their different levels of anxiety.
Some were blessed and some were not.
Who decided who was who and what they got?

Maybe someday we will be reborn a different thing—
a rich man or pauper's son or a bird that can sing.
Living in a totally different place with different ideals,
experiencing different dilemmas, sorrow, and thrills.
The lesson of course is maybe we should all try
to believe "There but for the grace of God go I."

Joe E. Buczek
Surfside Beach, SC

Who Am I? Where Am I? Why Do I Exist?

My Father named me Zandra, Defender of Humanity;
Mother preferred Ruby, a very precious Gem.?
Uncle John called me Tampa, his favorite cigar;
My help mate, he called me Black Honey.
He worshiped the ground I walked on and gave me all his money.
Who am I? Where am I? Why do I exist?
Some call me Madam President, leader of EAAMA;
Others call me Madam Forman with the long arm of the law.
My name is Ruby Zandra Miller Stewart Waller; Sears' Teen Queen,
My two children call me mom. Society calls me Dr. of Education.
I even appeared in Ebony Magazine. I am a child of God living here on Earth.
 I exist because God and Gus loved me, and I loved them back.

Ruby Zandra Waller
Las Vegas, NV

I am author, poet, and earning my doctorate of education in organizational leadership with an emphasis in Christian ministry. I attend Grand Canyon University in Phoenix, Arizona. Writing poetry and prose helps to keep me balanced when my heart has been broken. I lost my husband of forty plus years on Memorial Day. My children are devastated, and we are all falling apart with grief. To make matters worse, social scecurity reclaim ed his social security and the pension specialist reclaimed our pension check. These funds supported our family while I am in school completing my doctorate.

White Glass on Black Eyes!

I saw them eating corn and mashed potatoes and reacted: poor people!
I saw them buying corns and mashed potatoes and reacted:
looks yummy man, from where did you buy, KFC!?
I saw them wearing slippers and reacted: poor and dirty people!
I saw them wearing slippers and reacted:
wow, it's cool man. From where did you buy, Timberland!?
I saw her wrapped in ripped clothes and reacted: poor girl!
I saw her buying ripped dresses and flashing her body and reacted:
you look so pretty and hot. Which brand, GUCCI!?
I saw them drunk and screaming and reacted: cheap people, no culture!
I saw them drunk and screaming "this is so f****** awesome man,"
and reacted: you are f****** right bro!
I saw them riding a bicycle and reacted: poor people!
I saw him renting a bicycle and reacted: cool man, being green han!?
I saw them defecating in an open environment and reacted:
poor and dirty people, so unhygienic, ewe!
I saw them...no...I didn't, I know they wipe their back with napkins and
reacted: new brand, soft, and extra size, from where did you buy!?
I saw him working at a gas station and ordered:
hey, fill the tank and no scratch on my car, okay?
I saw him working at a gas station and reacted: hey you lucky man,
got a job, see if you can find one for me!
I saw them socializing with family and friends and sleep quietly,
and reacted: idiots, ambitionless people!
I saw them chasing, broken family, lonely, and taking sleeping pills,
and reacted: ohh man, I'm tired, don't know how and where to find
peace!?
I don't know when and how I got a white glass on my black eyes!

Sushant K. Singh
Irvington, NJ

Where Is Wisdom

I've searched for wisdom near and far,
for oh so many years.
I've looked in libraries, book stores and flea market stalls.
I've lined my shelves with all the great works
and white papers by the bale.
I've answered ads citing "Wisdom For Sale"
all to no avail.
As hard as I try to make wisdom include me,
it always balks and eludes me.
It seems the closest I'll get to wisdom
is being a wise-guy.

Jacob E. Brown
LaPorte, IN

Creative World

Prisoners of emotions ready for release of empathy.
From the encyclopedia of chapters of life, permission given.
Seasons filled with memories running a race.
Like wind blown leaves across the yard.
Racing to see who will finish first in the Olympics of touching others hearts.
Tears flowing from the waterfalls of sensitivity.
Meals served with love to let others know I understand.
Love seeds planted to grow.
Watered with compassion and passion just so you know.
Poetry passports stamped so you can travel with the community
of poets and poetess of international and local origins.
Welcoming one and all to the exclusive soothing relaxing creative
world with smooth jazz playing to God be the glory!

Curtis R. Johnson, Towntaker Poet
Jackson, MS

Where Are We Going?

America is in a terrible crisis!
There is a war of words going on everywhere.
Political parties cannot work together.
Different races cannot tolerate each other.
I wonder if Americans will find ourselves.
I wonder what our forefathers would think.
We know how they worked hard to make us free.
Our forefathers paid a dear price—death and war.
Today, we have a lot to consider and think about.
Now, all citizens need to put our differences aside.
Politicians should really talk to each other, not yell!
They need to face the problems in America,
and they can work together to fix them.
What a difference that would be for all!
Everyone from the president to the poorest
would finally be treated with respect.
What are we going to choose to do?
It is time to start healing American's wounds!
Maybe then problems of racism, wars, and
unity will begin to be solved for all of us.
When the miracles of healing our nation work,
Americans can then hold our heads high again.
All we need to do is believe in America
and the journey one and all will travel to help her.
Are we ready to make America strong again?
"God bless America" again, now, and forever.

Martha Weller
Mora, MO

When You Go to Heaven

Is heaven as beautiful as they say
Is there sunshine warm and bright every day
Does fear and pain leave your body free
When you show up at the gate of eternity
Are there angels there to greet your soul
Does the Lord pick out your new role
Are there classes to teach you heavenly things
Are pastels the color of angel's wings
Even though your memory is now just a dearth
Saddened are the ones left behind here on Earth
Will you get the chance to ask the reason why
God chose you now to dance in the sky
Life here on Earth can be so reckless
Have you lived in life's gracious essence
Do you love and give without exceptions
Have you conquered bad and evil obsessions
Does your life matter with responsibilities
Did you give into sin's susceptibilities
Did you master vices and addictions
In heaven are you free from those afflictions
Has faith guided the roads you chose
Did you trust that God absolutely knows
Did you believe you are in God's good hands
Cuz we never know exactly his plans
Life is beautiful in both places
Always give thanks and be gracious
Love is eternally honor bound
Hear its echo as your life's sound
So when your life here on Earth goes missing
And you're in heaven receiving God's blessing
Be thankful the Lord allowed your birth
Be humble and grateful for your life on Earth
You will never know the day you will leave!

Ladyann Elizabeth Graham-Gilreath
Miami, FL

I was in a car accident and my neck was broken and I thought I was going to die and while I was being worked on at the hospital, I started thinking if and why God has sent for me and why now? Had I lived the life I should have and was I a good person? Then I wondered what Heaven would be like.

When I Count My Blessings

When I count my blessings you are number one
I cannot believe it was your heart that I won
After all is said and done
We had a loving marriage and made a great son

When I count my blessings you are the best
You always made me the happiest
North, south, east, or west
You were always a notch above the rest

When I count my blessings that exist
You are at the top of the list
I have loved you since that first kiss
And I thank you for all our wedded bliss

Chester Williams
Jewett City, CT

Interwoven

Our lips are still moist
after our recent lover's embrace
While holding each other strongly
we feel each other's pulse
Our passions are aglow
Our pillow talks afterward
lead us to believe we are interwoven

Gavin J. Wahl
Long Beach, CA

I am a navy man, honorably discharged as a navy petty officer. I'm currently in a rehabilitation center recovering from a stroke. I was inspired to write by my high school literature teacher Paris Goodrun, T. S. Eliot, and writings and song lyrics of the sixties. This poem is dedicated to my friend Dewayne and his wife Summer.

What's a Poem?

What's a poem, if not a chance to roam headlong into my thoughts.
Free falling into words that no longer belong to anyone.
What's a poem, if not soaring above the expectant clouds.
What's a poem, if not a promise to love you forever and a day;
even if you're holding me back in the worst possible way.
What's a poem if not the sweetest gift to myself as a writer,
spontaneously flowing, unlike my fiction that savors unknowing.

Poem appears suddenly out of nowhere delighting in my emotion.
Tugging at something inside, kidnapping me like a lover's potion.
What's a poem if not the moment of truth, when I can be one…
With me. With you. With the Earth.
What's a poem, if not me longing for humanity to hold one another like
the sand and the sea.
What's a poem, if not taking the scenic route back home to me.

Debra L. Gish
Lake Alfred, FL

To Us

This morning light falls
gently and caressing

The clearest blue sky
holds the hand
of this beautiful earth

Overwhelmed
there is neither longing
nor things to do

Just being present
for this one moment
given to us

Paul Stephen Benson
St. Paul, MN

Whatever Comes

Whatever comes
Take it in stride,
Hop in the saddle,
Get on with the ride.
Do the right thing
Whatever it may be.
Lead with your heart,
Let your conscience be free.
Take the bull by the horns,
Play the game fair and square.
Let the dice roll no matter where.
So whatever the day unloads,
Meet it head on.
Meet the sunrise and sunset
Leaning upon the Lord.

Catherine Smith
Bumpass, VA

Believe Your Dream

Yes, there *will be lights* burning brighter somewhere,
Even if things look dark and dim out there;
Freedom, liberty and humanitarian kindness
will place a smile on everyone's face
in this sometime raining sad world and place
a serene and happy glowing faithful fearless face, like fine lace;
We'll find that warmer land
Where all of us brothers will walk together, as we hold someone's hand,
and the dream, yes, the dream will truly come true
A Peaceful Refuge where birds highly fly
And all the people look out toward the gentle blue rainbow sky
And even if outside negative bad sources try to break us,
Turn out our lights, our human spirit won't give up the fight
Our hearts will ignite to our heavenly forces all night
Yes, our dream can come true, yes, our dream can come true
There will always be a candle in answer to your righteous question
A promise that will take away "all doubts and fears no matter how far or near"
We'll no longer be trapped in a world full of pain
Dr. King, JFK, RFK, did not die in vain
No one will separate us ever again
While we can still stand in this proud land
We shall never fall, for our hearts and our spirits will
eternally sing, "May liberty always reign tall,
May human dignity be our never-ending call
May we always stop to think and slowly talk:
For this dream is truly for one and all
This dream is for one and all
"Let your dream come true right now"!

Mary Alice Peña-López
San Antonio, TX

Mary Alice Pena-Lopez lives in San Antonio, TX, with her husband of twenty-seven years Jaime. Mary teaches Kinder school and Jaime works in an art museum. My inspiration is based on the song "If I Can Dream" sung by Elvis Presley; it is a song that raises many questions about the world we live in. It was sung more than thirty-five years ago yet it is as relevant today as ever. I hope people will listen to the song, read my poem, and know that our spiritual lights, hopes, and dreams will never die. Good will always win over evil! Love will never be killed or murdered!

What You See!

Light becomes form and returns to light
Shadow and substance interchange
Light fractured in images familiar and strange
Glare becomes glow in the changing light.

That which is there is seen differently
And that which is not seen as well
My fractured view travels near then away
Reality—it's hard to tell.

I reach out to touch, to verify
With another sense what is real
All that is seen may still be there
Some just with an internal "feel."

Experience no longer a faithful gauge
Things change both inside and out
May that "feel" be of wonder and not of rage
Let joy be the "feel" that I shout.

Robert B. Aukerman
Centennial, CO

What Is Beautiful?

I write seeking to sow a seed of faith within myself
that I might grow to be able to convey
the beautiful promise of life that lies within us all
if allowed to surface and not left to fester and decay.
I write hoping my pen will not just scratch the surface
but will penetrate deep into the heart
to release the beautiful feeling of joy
that kindness to and love of one another can impart.
I write inscribing a vision of peace and harmony
to bring into focus how beautiful the world could be.
If we could revel in knowing our children are safe
and that all the children of the world are free.
I write acknowledging the revelation
that has been a long time coming
to realize that the many blessings
we receive outweigh the strife.
To appreciate the beautiful scenery we encounter
as we get tossed on the fast-paced
and tumultuous roller coaster of life.

Jane F. Bass
Smithville, TN

Sane of Insane

Ink spots
Ink blotches
They are one
Not the same
One is an accident
The other determines
Whether you are
Insane
Psychologically over-medicated
Confused thoughts
Rule the day night
Impulsive produced self suggestion
To know prove to know not
Exhausted emotionally drained
We aimlessly stumble
Into the endless bottomless pit
Spiraling out of control
Ever searching for insanity's
Sanity

Milton E. Morrow
Milwaukee, WI

What I Asked Jesus For

This Christmas
I asked Jesus for joy
For every single
girl and boy
I asked Jesus for hope
In these disturbing times
So we can all cope
I asked Jesus for love
To be sent to all
From the good Lord above
I asked Jesus for peace
That all wars in the world
Will abruptly cease
I asked Jesus to hear what I pray
That He please send the above
Every day
I asked Jesus for forgiveness
And I gave Him
Humility and my thankfulness
Then I asked Jesus for mercy
That He will help me
To be all I can be

Saundra Russell
Tucson, AZ

What Can You Do?

Teach the hands
that will slowly grow
Lead the footsteps
but let them choose the path to go
Mend the hearts of the broken
so they can love again
Believe in the goals
so they never give up but be certain
Fill the minds with imagination
to create wonders of their own
Instruct the skills needed
that they will continue to hone
Tend the wounds
but allow there to be something learned
Assist with the endeavors
so they understand what is earned
Form the bond
that provides a connection
Encourage their best
without demanding perfection
Chase away the doubts
in order to help them keep their dreams
Guide the curiosity
to discover themselves what life means

Kayla Evans
Wayne, MI

Bumblebees

In spring, when my linden tree flowers,
they cover the delicate clusters of blooms
like a blanket, fat one-inch-long critters
of buzzing intensity, hanging it seems,
from virtually every source of nectar
and draining its microscopic sweetness
before hum-buzzing on to the next cluster.

As a boy, those big black buggers
terrified me. They still do, raising
the hackles on back of my neck.
Hornets do, too, having been stung
rapid-fire as a young'un by squadrons
of enraged inhabitants of a nest
I was foolishly bombarding with rocks.

But back to the bumblebees—
or rather, the honeybees.
Whatever happened to those kindly critters
you'd kick up from clover blooms
when racing across fields as a kid?
They're outnumbered at least ten-to-one
by bumblebees on my linden tree!
Are weed killers decimating the clover?
Or is it simply that, in today's world,
the bigger and stronger must always win out?

I hope not, because I still dislike bumblebees.
And hornets.

Joseph H. Kempf
Indianapolis, IN

Seventy-nine and still going strong! God is indeed good!

Unsocial Media

I'm here on a tablet, I'm there on a phone
24/7 and still I'm alone
10,000 followers, I'm hoping for more
But sometimes I cry out, what's all of this for?
Am I that lonely, am I that insecure?
I think I have friends, but can I be sure?
It's not like they ever come over and visit
I look in the mirror and wonder, what is it?
What is it that wakes me deep into the night?
What is it that shakes me and fills me with fright?
What is it that grips me and claws at my heart?
What is it that rips me and tears me apart?
Fear that I'll die and leave nothing behind?
You know what they say: out of sight, out of mind
Somebody else to be taking my place
With a different name and a different face
Facebook and Twitter, Snapchat, Instagram
They all have me thinking about who I am
A star of the now, a fresh online presence?
Or, 12 months from now, unplanned obsolescence?

Clinton Sells
Sarasota, FL

Unity

The unity we're feeling now, we should feel every day
God's love should flow in all our hearts as we bow down and pray

The Lord wants us to get along, to love, and to respect
Helping neighbors and our friends and those we haven't met

It doesn't matter where we go to church or where we pray
If we know Jesus died for us and that He is the way

We're bound together by His blood, whatever tint of skin
No matter height or language spoke, we all belong to Him

The unity in this place should spread the whole world through
With love and joy and peace and hope He'll fill our hearts anew

We each are children of our God; He loves us all the same
Way before we're in the womb, He knew us each by name

So spread His love as you move around to everyone you see
His Love's enough to get us through to live in unity

Pamela J. Yohn
Kokomo, IN

Truth

Look in the world
What do you see
People, who are not what they seem

Everyone lost
In a world they create
Not knowing what is real or fake

We live in a time
Where freedom is
But people still hide in darkness

Few will show
The truth of life
But most will only show the false.

Madison Humphries
Salisbury, NC

This poem is about the world around us. None of us are what we claim, but few of us will admit it.

Love Has Many Colors

My darling mother died when she was forty-five
A peaceful time till death arrived
We talked, laughed, and cried...
She wrote a note: Thanks, it is my life!

This is her life:
Her hair was long and flaming red
Her lips and nails, her body was perfect
Red roses filled her room...

A perfect secret no one knew
A business that she clearly loved
Love... has many colors
Red roses filled her room!

I could not do what she did so well
I worked from nine to five and when I came home
She was alive and beautiful
Red roses filled her room...

Celebrating love...
They all came to sing the last song
Who am I to judge? After all
It was her life...
Red roses filled her grave!

Helga Gross
Amargosa Valley, NV

To the Memory of My Gardening Mother

Deeping red gladioli
Brilliant yellow roses
Pure white geraniums

Now gone
replaced by
curly lettuce, cherry tomatoes
sweet onions, purple kale
good healthful all

The living lively fragrances
the beauty of
these vibrant plants

Bring long suppressed
memories of my frail thin
gardening mother

Her bright lovely flower bed
then her gleaming
vegetable patch
her gentle nurture of cats
stray and suffering
her devoted feeding of
birds colorful or drab

Her dogged determined
Honor of nature and
All life
these bittersweet memories
Break my Heart

Eleanor Shannon Lee Blakeny
New York, NY

To Logan and Bexley

Hi Logan Alan and Bexley Quinn
I love you both, you are my kin
But more than that, you are my friend
So far away, so many miles apart
It's difficult to visit
But you are always in my heart
Close your eyes and visualize
My presence in the room
I'm in the air, I'm everywhere
And I hope to see you soon
One day your mom will read to you
This poem that I wrote
And maybe both of you will visit
Before you are old enough to vote
You are both connected
By having a stroke at birth
But never let that diminish your worth
Great things you can achieve
If only you will believe
Love, Pop

W. V. Sadler
Powhatan, VA

To Behold Beauty

Delightful, satisfying love
manifests itself in many splendorous ways.
Love portrays in all its goodness.
When you do yourself well,
you can do somebody else.
Nestled in each heart
illuminating lights of love from Heaven above.
And when paired with kindness from every corner
of the world, surrounded sweetness.
Love is precious every time in time.
To warm your world with love, grace, and brilliant beauty.
This is a joy to behold, felt forevermore.
All around the world in a brilliant light of God's love.
Love portrayed in all its goodness here, there, and everywhere
gently turning the world with your love,
grace of beauty, crown of glory, love deeper
than the deep blue sea.
Heavenly divine, love shining so bright, both day and night,
for the love of love beloved.
Embrace the world with love.
Love's mighty warmth glows worldwide.
Love fame forever and ever, everlasting love.
Spectacular beauty paired with kindness,
unique and sweet.
You can create a wonderful world with your love
from Heaven above.

Mae Nell James
Dearborn, MI

Time Traveler

Old Elijah was a time traveler; I do believe.
First you see him then you don't.
In and out of heaven and earth,
              where he goes, no one knows.
With great speed, in the blink of an eye, there he would be,
              up on a mountain top or down in the valley.
He was moved by the spirit of God; they claimed.
Fed by the Ravens of the air they all declared,
       he fearlessly and suddenly would appeared out of no where!
Old Elijah never saw the inside of a grave,
      taken up in lighting speed; witnessed by his friends,
           abducted by aliens or angelic beings?
Alternating in and out of thin air, he just disappeared in a Chariot of fire,
Whirling, whirling, whirling, the mighty winds aspired to take him higher and higher.

Alisha Beauchamp-Boettger
New Braunfels, TX

Time Served in Battle

Early evening I watch the treeline before me through my window
and I spot the trickling fog pass by the trees.
Silent. A graveyard at midnight.
The smooth white flowing forward like a wall of crushing froth
from the bellowing current following from behind.
With it comes the screaming cold on the night's air, making my
skin crawl, raising my hairs throughout my body.
I hear, then, the sound of battle and its voices.
Swords clashing and/or muskets firing. Black powdered cannons
booming.
Thousands of men roaring, crying out to war.
Harsh whispers. Begging pleas. Children crying out in the distance.
Voices I thought were long gone now reappear in the mystic,
ghostly scene.
I watch, mesmerized, as this lost field
has reanimated outside my window.
Showing me. Speaking to me.
I then came to understand the event before my very eyes
for all the veterans we've lost in that past life.
I salute those who have served and fallen in battle/war
in the past and to the present.
Thank you for serving and honoring your most important code:
protecting the people and our homeland.

Ezekiel J. Watkins
Renton, WA

This Old House I Inherited

Call the city about this old house I inherited.
A leaky roof, my tenant's new furniture—call the city.
Termites are eating this old house—call the city.
The landscape is destroyed by the tenant who shuts off the water
—call the city.
The house is not up to code—call the city.
Thirty days to bring this house up to code—call the city.
Plumbing is old—call the city.
Fix the pipes—call the city.
Electrical is not up to code—call the city.
Cuban tenant call the city.
A crack in the foundation—call the city.
Field mice crawling and running in the house—call the city.
This old house I inherited is all fixed
Thanks to His Print Ministries.

Monica Sherlock
Carpinteria, CA

Then and Now

What fools that we may be
Yes, we look, but do not see
All the warnings, all the signs
We do not let it cross our minds
Yes, we listen, but do not hear
If we did, then there'd be fear
Of what, where, who, and how
When will they strike, will it be now
Remember all those years ago
We were met by deadly foe
Those who lost their lives that day
Did they know, what did they say
Will this happen yet again
Not knowing how or even when
Look and see, listen and hear
Pay attention, but not with fear
Never hide out or stay in
Because if you do, then they win
Never forget, always remember
2001, the 11th of September

Debra Russom
Naples, FL

Then and Now

It seems so strange now where I grew up
With kids of many hues and shades.
It never made no difference to any of us
As long as you could play a game.

Our neighbors were raised together,
Grade school to college, then marriage.
We made passionate love to our husbands,
Bringing a new life into our baby carriage.

Our wonderful background was family,
Love for each other, and caring.
Work, school and playing six days,
As Sundays were for praying and sharing.

Being "socially correct" seems to be the norm,
But I ask you, when did it occur and why?
As you are only hurting your family and friends
To continue to behave in this way.

It's not too late to start to change.
If everyone agrees to do the same,
"Love thy neighbor as thyself"
Soon your life won't be a "game."

Dottie A. Vaughn
Yuma, AZ

The Words We Speak

Have you ever thought of the words we speak?
Then have power of life and death, we're told.
Yet they're spoken by a tongue that's so very small.
We are amazed it can be so bold!

And the pain they cause can last so long.
We wonder, "Will they ever go away?"
Will they remove the hurt they have caused?
Pray hard they will and will not stay!

One other thing we should never forget—
A word fitly spoken is like this,
"Apples of gold in settings of silver"
Will restore all the joy and bliss.

Dear God, please choose the words that we speak.
May they never bring to anyone a tear.
We know if they come from your heart of love,
Then we will have nothing to fear.

Let us think long and hard before speaking,
Then use words that bring life to all.
Let the prayer of our heart then be simply
Put our tongues under your control.

Margaret Tew
Durham, NC

The Visitation

She married him after only four months.
It must have been around 1950.
Her parents didn't approve of Ed.
He owned the tavern in Humbird;
There's not even a sewage system.
On one clear day in June they eloped.
But decently, in the Lutheran Church.
Bev had been raised Presbyterian.
Ed later started his own business.
Theirs was a good, if prosaic life.
Bev is my mom's only living relative—
mom's first cousin.
Bev and Ed retired, like so many, in Florida.
When Ed passed away, I didn't tell my mom.
I didn't tell her that her cousin had become a widow.
That's because mom now lives in a memory care residence.
At Ed's visitation, I tried to fill in for my mom's absence.
We sat together, my first cousin, once removed, and I.
That's the term for such a relative—first cousin, once removed.
And yet, there Bev sat while my mom was absent.
Removed? It was hard for Bev to lose Ed.
It's also hard to accept who my mom has become.
If you listen at a visitation, it's hard not to learn something.
Bev had also learned something at a previous visitation.
Bev learned something at her own mother's visitation decades before.
Bev learned that she and her mother had, in fact, both been married
in that the same Lutheran Church.

Lisa Hill
St. Petersburg, FL

The Unwound Thread

From the beginning,
it was always about
changing who I was.

As a newborn I crawled
along and felt starved
through timeless ages.

I was always hungry,
and I loved the leafy green
leaves in life's sweet garden.

I became plump through my
endless eating. I was tired
and I wanted sleep.

I made a bed from silk, and
began to dream about flying
through endless meadows.

Beyond my dreams I awoke
spread my bright wings to
fly from blossom to bloom.

Ron Peat
Auburn, CA

R. H. Peat is seventy-seven and lives in the California foothills of the Sierra Nevada Mountains; he's been published in the USA, New Zealand, India, England, Canada, and Japan. He's operated open mics, poetry readings through Poet's & Writers, and taught poetry workshops. He's published in anthologies on a regular basis each year. He has a published book entitled, Abyss of the Moon (LCCN # 2010909546). He has won awards for his poems in many competitions. He also operates a closed workshop forum on the internet at Writing Forums, (.com) which has an international group of poems from different locations around the world including Australia, England, Canada, Holland, and India.

The Universal Cry for Help

I need help.
I am lost.
Trapped in the dark.
Someone find the switch before I find a knife.

I need help.
I'm drowning.
Can't come up for air.
Someone pull me out before it's too late.

I need help.
It's in me.
Can't get it out.
Someone do something before I fall asleep.

I need help.
The fog grows thicker.
Lines are beginning to blur.
Someone kiss me goodbye before I give up on life.

Shannon White
Santee, CA

The Times We Live In

Perfection of means and confusion of ends,
A condition that never mends,
But in the gray of the morning,
My mind becomes confused,
Between the dead and the sleeping
And the road that I must choose.
Casualty of the quixotic vicissitudes of predetermination,
Holding on to meaningless possessions with extreme
adoration,
Like a dying man clinging to an ebbing life of desperation.
Kismet, karma, fate and expectation, lead me to my destination,
Always ready for confrontation, surrendering
the futile concept of reconciliation,
Born free but always in chains, looking for someone for dreams to
exchange,
even though that may be out of my range.
I believe one day, that will bring abrupt change.

Constantine Liagouris
Piscataway, NJ

I'm Constantine, love poetry and Lord Byron, trying to assimilate in a world I don't recognize.

The Things You Say to Me

The words that come out of your mouth
Are meaningless and bland
You try to make me see
But they are worth less than every grain of sand
The things you say to me
Are heartless and cold
Every promise broken
Every lie ever told
The words you speak
Are poisonous ad weak
But yet I fall for them every time
Every sentence every rhyme
The things you say to me
Can me nothing less
Than heartache
A heartache I caress
I try not the listen
But the words get in
Breaking me down even more
You'd think it be a sin
The things you say to me
I no longer hear
I am a strong woman
And your words I no longer fear

Nickole Caryn Robinson
Las Vegas, NV

The meaning behind this poem is it's talking about a woman being degraded by all of the men in her life and she keeps listening to them, their words constantly hurting her and bringing her down. But one day she had finally had enough and decided to stop listening. She realized she was stronger than their words.

The Shell

With peace of mind you walk the sand,
You stoop, straight-legged, and grasp an island.
Unto itself this magnificent creation lives.
A spiral of life?
No straight thoroughfares, only bends and curves,
Blind corners, unknown 'til turned.
Five hundred million years of beauty.

With peace of mind you walk the sand,
You stop, chin high, with life in hand
And turn toward the promised land.
This life you hold is precious.
Hard shelled? Perhaps, but soft and warm and live.
You place it in the watery womb.
Five hundred million years of beauty.

With peace of mind you walk the sand,
You think, eyes timeless, of thwarted, sandaled feet
And smile inside for moth and man.
A myriad memories like walked on grains
Fill your heart and limbs and brain
'cause you have seen and felt and touched
Five hundred million years of beauty.

Fay Brett
Naples, FL

The Right to Exist

It has been said that physicians play God
That such life and death power is held precariously
within their hands, a virtual hour glass measuring
the sand of life.... Doctors solemnly adhere to
the Hippocratic Oath, which dictates first do no harm
yet violates said oath in cold cruel clinical fashion
as sterile robotic sociopathic abortionists.
Countless casualties in a different agenda of war
in which potential mothers are deceived, the innocent
lives of infants lost... denied a protective family,
the joys of a whimsical nostalgic childhood, the
security of the unconditional love of loyal pets.
Becoming a student of academia, embarking upon
a spiritual path of learning inspiration, wisdom,
seeking a soulmate to travel life's journey with...
partners in overcoming sorrow aspiring for a bright tomorrow.
Knowing the sweetly steadfast love of Christ Jesus
who "sticketh closer than a brother," His ocean deep
compassion like that of no other.
This according to our heavenly Father's plan, for His
design is exclusive, hauntingly beautiful as architect
and artist of every universe and all residing within...
of living, thriving, knowing the hope of a unique future.
Not dying in lieu of being born, never adorned,
never given the chance to exist;
life interrupted via the icy hands of the abortionists.

Jill J. Shaw
Saint Joseph, MO

The Old You

Whatever happened to the old you?
The one I genuinely fell in love with years ago.
The one with the sense of adventure in his eyes.
Always having a smile on his face instead of a frown.
Bring him back 'cause I'm bored sitting here alone,
Waiting for our lives to resume before you changed.
From morning till night, you're always on my mind,
Bringing sunshine back to my once isolated world.
Now I want to restore the light locked in your soul,
Rekindle the spark in your heart to burn radiantly.
I want to make you shine like a star in the night sky.
Let me be the one to silence the chaos in your life.
Whatever happened to the old you?
The one who stayed positive through the roughest storm.
The one who wiped his tears away every time he cried.
Always in high spirits even when you wanted to scream.
Bring him back 'cause I'm missing you as the days pass.
I've reached my paradise after giving you my heart.
The one object I was afraid to let go, even to you.
Since you uncovered my eyes from the darkness inside
You made me smile again after my world was torn apart.
You gave a new meaning to the emotion known as love.
You're the reason I want to move forward in this life.
Time has changed you and we've grown older in years
Yet my love continues to flow since the day we met.
So please let me be the reason the old you returns....

Roberto Cocina
Madison, AL

The Mystery of the Easter Card

In April I mailed an Easter card
To my pastor and his family.
In the card I put a twenty-dollar bill,
And wrote *P.S. Don't give up on me.*
Low and behold, six months later,
The card, without an envelope whatsoever,
And no return address
Appears in my mailbox on a Saturday in October.
I opened the card and there was the same twenty
I had put inside the card.
The reason I knew it was the same twenty
Because on the edge was the blue ink.
I had not been to church in four years
Since my beloved husband passed away.
I didn't think I could go and hold back the tears
But I knew I had to go back someday.
When I think of how many hands the card was touched by
How many could have used that twenty,
It brings tears to my eyes a plenty.
I truly believe with all my heart
God had a hand in this from the start.
Needless to say, the very next day,
I went to church and gave pastor his card, money intact.
This is a true story in fact.
God does work in mysterious ways;
That's all I have to say.

Rebecca M. Roach
Altamonte Springs, FL

Whispers in the Dark

In this moment...
Silence.
Spaces in between.
Gravity pulling.
And yet unafraid, as hearts open.
This vulnerability in this beauty, but weak, while fingertips crawl...
Keen eyes.
Dark place, hidden secrets, behind closed walls.

Benita Lashae Priestley
Seaside, CA

The Memories Linger

Sixty years ago my parents bought our family home,
In a town that to all of us was unknown.
I was seventeen, a senior in high school,
Trying to live by the golden rule.
There were twelve of us kids plus Mom and Dad.
We all grew up through the good and bad.
Marriages, deaths, birthdays, the usual highs and lows—
This is how the scheme of life goes.
I was the last to marry and moved away,
But two brothers and a sister stayed.
The years rolled by, my husband became sick,
He was rushed to the hospital real quick.
He slipped into a coma and was soon gone.
I knew I had to go forward and move along.

Winifred J. Love
Abington, MA

Memories

Standing in dry Cranberry Bogs.
Rows and rows of Tomato Plants.
A shed full of tools.
Marathons of World War Two movies.
A dark green truck with a camper shell.
Important life lessons.
Janice Joplin songs.
A lifetime washed in alcohol.

Joelle Margarete
Fairfield, CA

The Kings of Fashion

American who, what or wear
Brash as hell and just don't care
Capital invest or ready to cash in
But don't forget the Kings of Fashion

Silk or satin? The facts are in
Leather or lace? Each has its place
Just match it with gems in the jewelry case
And don't forget the Kings of Fashion have a face

Wear in, wear out, or wear when out
Wear up, wear down, or wear without
Make no mistake about this American passion
This is serious business for the Kings of Fashion

Darryl Monteiro
Fall River, MA

The Hell of Cold War III

I became blue
when the military drafted you
and didn't know what to do!
When you were lost,
we paid the cost.
When I heard you died,
to not, I tried and tried,
but I just cried.
I remembered when you were born
and got incredibly torn.
Every single day
I noticed your own way.
You were a slightly different child
but seemed inspired.
Throughout your life,
you put out strife.
When you were born,
we couldn't be torn!
We loved you so
and hated when you had to go.
To Heaven you flew,
when the Vietnamese bombed you!

David A. Ott
Wapakoneta, OH

The Gods' Bellows Blow

The wind blew so intensely yesterday...
I envisioned a gigantic bellows—
wondering who might be at the helm of it in the universe,
imagining the long ago, infamous gods of Greek times
standing at a sacred pulpit
wielding a golden shift rod pressing the bellows,
emitting an intense air from their cauldron pit
as in a wake-up call to mankind.
In a quandary...
Did those Greek gods really vanish from the minds of men?
What if the minds of men went into reverse?
More thinking of those Greek gods of the universe...
What if "God" was really Zeus, the controller of all men?
Like a chess board piece, Zeus, maneuvering the world.
The universe is vast, as well as the vastness of one's mind,
always searching to find some sort of an answer,
constantly searching for why we're here on Earth...
How *did* we really come to exist?
The winds of change—
a god's warm breath bellowing through the lips of them?
Mount Olympus is where they used to dwell.
In that era there was no Heaven or Hell.
No, as above, so below (in Tantric)

Nancy L. Cox
Denver, CO

The Girl Who Used to Be

I long for the girl who used to be
So full of life, so happy and free
So young in heart and spirit and soul
Never did she dream that she would grow old

Years seem to fly as this life she lived
Raising a family and learning to love and give
All that she could to the one's she held dear
But now they are gone, but once they were so near

Time is so precious, our days are so few
Why is it so hard to say I love you
Too late to undo the things she's done wrong
Time won't turn back, though for it we long

But I pray God will smile and understand, too
That we are just dust and try as we do
Mistakes are made; that we can't undo
Maybe someday, Lord, your children will see
The only life we can keep is a life lived for Thee

Helon Phillips
Cordesville, SC

Max

My heart followed behind you
every step of your passing,
my heart will forever remain
by your side where it belongs.
The echoes of your presence
resonates within my mind,
the emptiness around me
filled heavy with sadness.
What should I do now
for my life was yours,
now I am lost
in this endless grief.
I miss hearing your doggie steps
as you were my house shadow,
and seeing the tilt of your head
when asked to go out.
I miss the cuddles
that you knew I needed,
even your loud barking
I now wish to hear.
Thank you for always protecting Mama;
you are a good boy.
Now go run free until again we meet,
and together we will be for all eternity.
It's okay, you can go… it's okay,
Mama will be okay… Mama will be okay.

Judy Cennami
Portsmouth, NH

The Conversation

How do you know me, O Lord?
Before I formed you in the womb, I knew you. Jer. 1:5
As I lived my life, were you there?
Where can you go from My spirit?
Where can you go from My presence? Psalm 139:7
Did you take notice, how I lost my way?
The Son of Man came to seek and to save
what is lost. Luke 19:10
Where did you find me?
I redeemed your life from the pit . . . . Psalm 103:4
How do I get on the right path?
I am the way, the truth, and the life . . . . John 14:6
My Word is lamp to your feet and a light to your
path. Psalm 119:105
Who am I, O Lord?
You are a child of the Most High . . . . Luke 6:35
Now is the beginning of your journey with Me.

Marianne Gorman
Morrisonville, NY

The Bottle

I see my son.
No I don't.
My brown eyed babe is not here.
He is gone.

Years pass as years do and he grew.
There was a bottle.
Inside was clear liquid, like water.
But it wasn't.
Outside on the bottle was a large "V"
Like the first letter of the word "vodka".

He wanted what was inside.
Desperately.
It wanted him.
From the depths of my soul I cried "Stop! Stop!"
But he could not.
He drank all of it.

The bottle laughed at me.
It laughed at me as if to say, You!
You cannot win, you will not win.
And I didn't.
The bottle took him from me.

I see my son.
No I don't.
He is gone.

Forever

Jean B. Herbert
Clearwater, FL

The Body Beautiful

Upon awakening every morning
I gently stretch my limbs
Sounds much like a rusted organ
Cranking up to play a hymn

Stones have invaded my kidneys
Arthritis has settled in
I seem to be aching
From my toes up to my chin

My shoulders are sprouting bone spurs
Ripping up my rotator cuffs
I've had surgeries galore
Sometimes making me a little gruff

When I reached my fifties
Hot flashes ravaged me
My estrogen is being depleted
Adding night sweats to this melee

There is metal in my body
I have an artificial knee
Yet I wake up every morning
Still thanking God for blessing me

Laura P. Smith
Pinebluff, NC

Someone We Can Trust

Sometimes when I am all alone
And my misfortunes I bemoan
I think of all I've made it through
Focusing on all You would have me do
For the ways we are to go are in Your Word
Directions for life, promises kept, nothing absurd
Thank You, dear Lord, for all You have given us
But most of all for being the Someone we can trust
Without You we can do so much wrong
And with You we can always be so very strong

Martha Bond Branson
Macon, GA

The Beggar

Obsidian oblivion - warm and wet.
pressing on my palm while licking up my sweat.
Pinkish hues and an ancient inhalation
slobber on my fingers with jumps of jubilation.
Wiggling, waggles - wanting scratches and kisses,
an uncontrolled tail whacking with near-misses.
Primal instincts kick in when his favorite ball is thrown;
Socks find new homes in places I've never known.
Dash! Clunk! CRASH! Careening down dark corridors.
Skid! Bang! THUD! Running into creaky old doors.
Landing on my lap, wide eyes begging for rubs -
There is no greater feeling than a dog's love.

Friday Bakhos
Tustin, CA

Teacher Teacher

Karma is
The perfect teacher.
Patience is
Her greatest virtue
Teaching the same lessons
Over and over
In her perfectly-tailored
Classroom
Until we
Get them.
The lessons
We need to learn...
The Lessons of Life.

Sharon Etta Freeman
Eden Prairie, MN

State of War

We're in a war
we don't know we're in,
Against the father
of lies and sin.
Who taught this world
he does not exist,
So how can mortal men resist?
It's only by the Holy One
Who strengthens us
in all we do,
Negatting lies with what is true.
And in the end
we know we win,
This spiritual war
we all are in.

Jefferson Murphy
Milton, NY

Super Space

Dressed to be very weather tough,
Winter and summer are always rough.
Each and every one has a personality;
Long live the cabin under a willow tree.

Lounging around just about anywhere
Into a forest or a concrete thoroughfare.
Neatly dressed for whatever location,
Getting a bungalow or cottage for vacation.

So all is well in mansions, condos, or towns.
Are real ranches and farms for working clowns?
Remember some places are someone's big fix—
Every house, chalet, manor, villa, or duplex.

Hence our place is our home sweet home;
Our mobile really doesn't have a glass dome.
Most others prefer flats, lofts, or huts,
Ending in the doghouse will always be too much.

Still last but not least you will see
Houses that can be beach, tent, or teepee.
Echoes of safe havens all over the land,
Looking sick, these old shacks still stand.

There's a spot where you can hang your hat,
Even at the front door there's a welcome mat.
Relaxing after your shoes are tossed aside,
Super space to return to with some pride.

Harry J. Russell
West Seneca, NY

My Mother Was Younger Than Me

My mother was born in 1920 and Letha was her name.
Being a baby born in leap year brought her some fame!
If Mother Letha today was still here
she would have reached her twenty-fifth year.
Many times during her life she would comment to me:
You will always be much older than your mother, you'll see!
Mother would have her twenty-fifth birthday February 29th this year
and on March 31st I, her daughter, will celebrate seventy-nine, I fear.
Who was my mother?
She was a woman far ahead of her time and
at such a young age, she certainly did shine.
She managed the Sherman Theater throughout the 1950s
and a Pennsylvania State Employment Agency in the 1960s.
I was born when my mother was only five.
Oh how I wish she was still alive.
Mother Letha left this world at the age of twenty years.
But the memory of her shines bright through my tears.
My mother will be remembered and cherished every day
but people will never understand when I say:
My mother was younger than me!

Letitia M. Lladoc
Stroudsburg, PA

Spider Lilies

While hunting Wild Turkeys I saw them there;
wild Spider Lilies with blooms yet to bare.
Prominent green plants in our Mississippi nation,
readying themselves for a summer celebration.

I shared my good news with Ginger my wife.
We both find joy in the outdoor life.
Together we waited for their expected bloom,
then planned our visit to their outdoor room.

It's now mid-July, humid and hot.
We search out an area which I have not forgot.
The early morning quiet is all around,
so our search proceeds in peaceful surround.

Anticipation accompanies us while we seek,
in a hardwood bottom near Goodwater Creek.
A canopy of oaks and hickories, too,
form an outdoor cathedral welcoming two.

Soon we find them in their annual bloom,
magnifying God in their outdoor room.
Delicate white flowers crowning a green leafless stem,
with their spider-like appearance designed by Him.

So here we stand in this special place;
these lilies of God have smiled our face.
Their July occurrence ever amazes the mind;
creation treasures that are a joy to find.

James H. Bryant Jr.
Bay Springs, MS

Something to Look For

Lord please help me climb this hill,
Help me find some happiness.
I have a bit of time left still,
Despite the swiftly passing years.

Until that fateful day
I have had a happy life as
My poems seem to say,
Then came the day when happiness just went away,

I'm living in this empty shell
Empty, sad and lonely all the time
It hurts to view the life before and
There is no life ahead that's mine.

Came the day we had to leave
The good life back on the farm.
'Tis to this little farm
That my heart still only sees.

I know I must find a way
To bring the happiness back.
Surely there is something here
That can ease the painful lack.

Leanora Salmon
Sebastian, FL

Snow Melts My Heart

Standing on the mountain
looking down upon my town
The house that we shared as one
where memories are filled wall-to-wall

Snow started falling where I stood
and the town far below
I feel the snow melting
on this lonely heart of mine

I felt warm in the snow
I'm surrounded by cold and wind
There was a feeling of being hugged
I looked down and saw footprints in the snow

Your presence I feel whenever I'm blue
my heart feels the snow melting
when it touches my mind and soul
I am missing you, son, I love you

Jerry Yates
Jacksonville, AL

Shopping at the Ice Cream Store

Flavors of ice cream you may enjoy are vanilla, chocolate,
strawberry, butter pecan, and cookies & Cream.
Ice cream holders are cones, bowls, or cups for a scoop or two.

Milkshakes may be made from chocolate, vanilla, and
strawberry ice cream or even pineapple or peppermint.
Malts have germinated cereal grain but milkshakes don't.
Floats are made with ice cream, cheerwine, Coke, or ginger ale
and taste good particularly in the summertime.

Mango sherbet uses pumpkin juice for its orange color
and a top ice cream brand that makes this is Haagan-Dazs.
Other popular brands of ice cream are Ben & Jerry's,
Breyers, Cold Stone, Edy's, Klondike, Pet & Sealtest.
Orange, lime, pineapple, and rainbow sherbet are
lighter and creamier than their sorbet cousins.

Banana splits and ice cream sundaes are delicious
favorites at ice cream soda shops especially with
syrup, nuts, whipped cream, and a cherry on top.

The marvelous invention of ice cream was introduced
in 1904 at the World's Fair in St. Louis, Missouri.
It's been a popular dessert choice for over a hundred years.
Yum, yum for these delicious treats!

Ralph Whitley
Concord, NC

She Is

She is hot
She is sexy
She is sweet
She is as the french would say exquisite
She beautiful, brilliant
She is a star
She walks like a model
She speaks eloquently
She is a dream come true
She is enchanting and charismatic
She has a smile that lights up the world
She is class
She is kind and loyal
She is a friend
She is everything
She is a woman
She is charming and breathtaking
She has my hearty, soul and spirit
She is stunning, eclectic and an artist extraordinaire
She is music and the beauty of nature
She is a rainbow she is a woman fascinating and mysterious
She is bbhs
You

Jo Ann Granello
Springfield, PA

Shadows of the Past

Our ancestors of old did what they could
If they stood tall, we heard and understood
Talk of them we do with spirits of glee
For we know who they were and forever will they be
In our hearts, woven to stay, their fortitude for living
Exemplary figures showing us a way of enduring
Troubles they had—as all who live have their turn
They showed us how—giving us lessons to learn
If we look to blame our circumstances at their cost
We would be making an error
And our feet standing would be lost
We make our own house from the bricks on hand
Though kin material is known
It is up to us to map the land
For if the right plan on a proven path is followed
Then ancestors' lives have value
And our path of existence gives credence to virtue
Therefore, shadows of the past
Become real to us in the light
We can progress and advance
Knowing families endure the night
By becoming righteous learners
Taking these known kin to heart
We create records to follow us—then our posterity
Will add their part.

Douglas Hovik
St. George, UT

Senseless Chatter

Each day at work I try so hard
But all my thoughts are shattered;
For just across the aisle from me
There's continuous, senseless chatter.
Be still I say, stop that right now.
But do you think that matters?
It just goes on, and on, and on,
That useless, senseless chatter.
I would get mad, but that's no good;
I'd be like that old mad hatter
Who no doubt would try and try
To stem the tide
Of that useless, constant chatter.
I guess I'll have to stop and think
And ponder on the matter.
I've just got to find a way to stop
That useless, senseless chatter.

Vera M. Meney
Rochester, NY

Seething

Seething, deep within my veins
A river, a river of rage,
Cursing, my blood boils
Hot, hotter against this injustice.
I see his foot rise from the accelerator
And the deliberate slamming of the brake.
I see you thrown against the windshield.
I hear your helpless cry.
I feel the hurt as your head hits hard.
I see him shove you into the elevator,
His loud piercing voice harassing your gentleness.
Upstairs, his brute strength pushing you harshly,
You fall to the floor stunned and hurt.
He gets a knife, the steel glittering in the false light,
False as he is,
Smooth talker, forked tongue.
I fought so hard
To bring you into this world—dear "feet first" baby.
You were to be a beautiful ballerina,
Not his punching bag.
How dare he diminish your beauty?
This disgusting, self-centered, no-good man!
He doesn't know who he is
And the search is destroying you
And me.

Ann Lee Knutson
Northfield, MN

Doctor Patient Relationship

I feel sick
Something is not right
Dark will come to light
And what he will do with what he finds
Will be unknown in deep minds
I feel trapped
You are capable of leaving
Yet you are still captive
A mind full of memories
All the ones you wanted to forget
They eat you alive when you are alone
Then the voices taunt and torture you
"Why can you not forget the pain
Remember the beauty"
"The pain remained when beauty was absent"

Alexis Bowden
Lincolnton, NC

Through life, I believe we all face obstacles that we cannot bring ourselves to speak upon. I use writing as a release. Reality is what I need it to be in my poems; I hope others find their own release as well.

Sandwich Generation

You know that cookie we all love
crisp chocolate embossed on the bottom.
Like pop and grandma's sharp observations
thinking lines and smile lines
rules and memories etched in faces and heart.
But fragile too, their steps not always steady.
Looking to us, the glue, holding family together.

Consider that cookie on the top,
nature's reflection of the bottom,
brittle but endearing, sometimes it even breaks.
Like the son, learning to drive,
scowling and silent.
Or the daughter,
wired as tight as the guitar she strums.
The next minute they smile, laugh at the world
eyes bright ready, even anxious to join the parade.

Then there is that creamy, sweet, center
that keeps top and bottom together.
The generation between, twisted apart
when the young call or the elders need you.
Whom do you answer first, who needs you most?
We love them both, need their wisdom and patience.
Need their natural desire for adventure and strength.

At some point we're the cookie, sometimes the cream.

Nancy J. Heggem
Palatine, IL

Round and Round

Caught in a broken teacup.
Spinning dazed in an endless circle
'Round and 'round it goes
Stuck in a broken teacup.
What once was a perfect picture stretches into an endless blur
Vibrant colors of all imaginable merge into a dull monochrome
Trapped in a broken teacup.
Weighted to a rusted seat
Echoes faint in one ear yet no sound is truly heard
In a broken teacup.
Waiting for its untimely end
Yet with endless passing time,
no one cares to glance at the broken teacup
So it continues to go 'round and 'round
Spinning nauseatingly in a repetitive circle
Silhouettes blur with monochrome color
Uniformity fades away
All of us trapped
To each our own rusted seat
Unable to escape
Chained to a broken teacup.

Carsen Roe
Louisville, KY

Rock and Sand

When you stand with house of stone,
breakage takes both rock and bone;
when places dear fall overgrown,
and people fade, once strength and tone;
when pleasant days seem to have flown
with blissful moments seldom known:

There will be mansions by time not thrown—
no cracks, no creaks, not even a moan.
There will be gardens God's seed will own
where people bloom, where love is grown.
There will be eons, peacefully prone,
when old become young, when no one will groan.

But Rock and sand, Creator and loan,
these dwellers will have chosen the way God's shown.

Wayne Mitchell
Red Oak, TX

Pools

Dew
   on the leaf
hangs a little jewel
   spark—
trembles a wet star,
   catching light . . .

Joh Cambilargiu
Tooele, UT

Rested

I sit quietly amidst my memories
As my spirit takes flight o'er the trees
Listening to sweet tones birds sing
Hearing soft flutters of angels wing
Far beyond this orb Earth I soar
To a universe ne'er seen before.
Bright colors flood my rested mind
All pain and sorrow lost; left behind
And in this time of bliss unheard
From beyond I hear His whispered word
Telling me at last all I need to know…
How far I have come: how far I go
As to my worldly bonds back I descend
In the vast unknown I found a friend.

B. J. McKee
Charlotte, NC

Respect Life

When we wander the woods
and three the towns
We see the humans
all around

They have no regard
For our daily life
They have no feeling
For them we are only
Worthless wildlife

We are the squirrels, the fox and deer
'As we lay dead on the roads
Our spirits do not diminish
We are survivors untold

Humans destroy our habitat
They wish we were gone
So they can pour concrete
Even though it's wrong

All creatures should respect
Each other in this world
For we care all essential
Created by our Lord

So if you view a mammal
On our sacred land
Show him the respect
That all God's children demand

Hallette C. Dawson
Herndon, VA

Refugee

When asked what is your name
I replied it is refugee
And oh why is that?
The reason is I am a man who has lost his homeland to war
to escape away thousands of miles to find a secure place
with a sense of belonging and acceptance
Even in cold stormy weather, sickness, vomiting, and hunger I endured
It is my strong will and determination that encourage me to carry on
in seeking for a brighter future and promises
You see I came across to the land of great America
It embraced me with humility to open a new door with a greater
opportunity to rebuild for a prosperous life
in which I call a second home
Only to know that I must start from scratch with bare hands and feet
That was my goal and inspiration to witness my children live
and surpass me
It has given me the voice to speak, the freedom to express,
opportunity to look
How can I not be grateful? Indeed I am
So, when you see other refugees out there
do not judge me as I plead I have grown thick skin
to stand high and seize with every second chance
never to take anything for granted
When life is tough and knocks me down I carry myself back up and
stand tall and be tougher than life itself
I am humble to call myself an American
To learn the true value of freedom and its meaning
in a place that is a melting pot for multi-cultural diversity
For that I salute to you—the great America you are
in all we stand together

Hanh N. Chau
San Jose, CA

Quicksand

Money, toxicity, relationships, politics, health, work.
Hypocrites, depression, increases wealth
of a docile self-absorbed creature-like gel
proving its madness are angels from humble hell

Miserable blind spots are good baits for starvation that
gobble up bitterness foreshadowers of bitter sweet news
or leaving room for introspection uncaring reflections
shifting mindsets are second thoughts expressions

Lying, addicted procrastinator's gaze splinters rooted in brews
cynical universe making hate complainers' booze

Beaming, waist length suction, an inescapable polecat
cynically woke me up or did I sprawl pondering everyone
has suffocating, crushing problems or issues ask anyone

Pity, shame, nor tears can't keep quicksand from being itself
Its gooey, viscosity is scary waiting for the sea's swells
that shall surely surrender to the polecat's gel
again, proving its madness are true angels from humble hell

Bozana Belokosa
Pasadena, CA

Prayer Warriors

Strengthen your hearts
Trust in God
Raise your eyes
Ignite your minds
Value one another
Empower yourselves

Face the future
Order your lives
Ride for the Lord

Give of yourselves
Own God's promises
Dare to believe

Catherine A. Ezzell
Bryan, TX

Pass Me By

I walk
you just pass me by
I walk in the cold weather
You just pass me by
I walk in the smothering heat
You just pass me by
I walk in the rain
You just pass me by
So I have only one request for you
When I lay dead in my casket
Don't let a single
tear fall from your eye
Just do what you did when
I was alive and pass me by

Debbie Toliver
Rotan, TX

Petrified

It's like all the answers you thought were right are wrong
The wind knocked out of you
The rug pulled out from under you
My whole world turned upside down and inside out
What, how am I supposed to go on like this?
What is the next step in the abyss of confusion?
What am I supposed to do?
And it's like out of f***ing nowhere
Kind of like the lines just thinned more and more,
until they were finally crossed
Like the bar just got so low
I finally stepped over
And now I feel like I'm in the deep end and don't know
how to swim
My head under water
Gulping for air
Gulping for truth
What is truth anymore?
What he says? What she says?
What this rabbi says? What this priest says?
What's even true in this world?
What's true for me? What do I want? Really? What do I want?
Breathe, you're alive
You're here for a purpose, I think?
I stand here on the precipice of some kind of life changing
moment
My foot dangling over the edge
And I'm petrified.

Yaffa Erica Slurzberg
Brooklyn, NY

Emotions of Poetry

Poetry could be the key to the mystery of how words
and thoughts come together to express wonder that
sometimes in a rhyming state of mind can confer.
Poetry can tell a story and tug at our emotions.
It can make us recall the peace of a misty midnight
meadow lighted only by the moon's gentle beams.
Poetry can also bring us tears as we wander through
a lifetime of memories of those whose paths we've
crossed, precious friends we've loved and lost.
Poetry should be many things to many people.
It should make us laugh. It should at times make us cry.
For it is said, "Kind words spoken to those in need
dry the tears of those who grieve."

James Harwood
Spencer, WI

I was inspired to write this poem by wondering how weaving together words and phrases can trigger an emotional response in the person who reads it, be it happy or sad or just brings back a memory from the distant past. I served in the US Army from 1966–1968. My hobbies include poetry, vintage electronics, and radios.

Pain

Pain, you're not my friend.
You push Pleasure off her pedestal
And show me lessons I never wished to learn:
Perseverance, humility and patience.
You know whenever I want something, I want it now!
I wear pride like a badge for all to see.
Facing difficulty, I'd rather do something else.

Pain, I am so tired of you, go away!
What did you say, without you I'd be numb?
Life and love diminishing in my search for Pleasure.
What was that? She is a fickle lover?
You say set my heart on higher things.
Do you mean the virtues that cost me time?

Pain, my teacher, I still don't like you.
I respect your task and surrender to the ordeal,
A prize of freedom from self; a priceless lesson.
So I love you? Only if that love deactivates fear,
Restores the power from heaven,
And my wrong thinking is replaced with a sound mind,
Then Pain, thank you.

Carol Welty Roper
Chugiak, AK

Midwestern Sunset

Driving westward into the sun,
A huge ball of fire hanging above a blue cloud.
Astonishing, I could not look away.
A lone blue peak appeared inside that red circle.
Looked like the Lone Cone.
as the sun dropped behind the clouds.

A second peak appeared.
reminding me of Wyoming's Tetons Range.
Those lovely, lonely Rocky Mountains.

Lee Lumpkins
Foristell, MO

Our Golden Wedding (1969–2019)

Being married to each other now for fifty years
In which we as husband and wife live a simple life together.
Whether it is sunny or raining.
We always have a harmonious behavior with each other.
Whether we are healthy or getting sick
We take good care of each other heart and soul.
Human life is full of difficulties
We try to forget ourselves in helping each other.
The emotions and duty of husband and wife are profound
We are patiently faithful in love to each other with perfection.
Thank you, almighty God, for granting us this favor
As we subsist in a happy and peaceful existence
Throughout our life…

Minh-Vien Nguyen
San Francisco, CA

Pieces of My Heart

You stole a kiss the day we met, it gave me a start.
You stole a kiss, and you stole a piece of my heart.
You took me on a date; I found I liked being with you.
Here we go again; now I've lost piece number two.
You pushed me high in the swing; I felt to wild and free.
Another piece of my heart; it's piece number three.
You sang a beautiful song to me; this song was "More."
I couldn't believe it, and I lost piece number four.
Whenever I'm with you, I feel so wonderfully alive.
Your kisses thrill me; there goes piece number five.
You loved to tease me; I loved all of your tricks.
Now that it's gone, I'll never miss piece number six.
Each time I'm with you, I feel like I'm in Heaven.
The pieces are bigger now; I lost chunk number seven.
You couldn't find a job; the army was your fate.
I'll be true, but I'll lose chunk number eight.
I read your letters and kiss each and every line.
I sure miss you, but I won't miss chunk number nine.
You write you are coming home; I'll see you again.
Here's the last piece; goodbye chunk number ten.
You now have all of my heart; it truly belongs to you.
You asked me to marry you—now I have your heart, too.

Janice Smith
Harrisonville, MO

When I met my future husband, it wasn't love at first sight. As we spent time together, I saw who he was and how we were together. Slowly but surely I fell in love with him. I dealt with his good points and learned his faults were few. After two years together we both knew we were right for each other. We were married forty-nine years and happy every step of the way. I believe "true love" takes time. You're really not prepared for it; it just sneaks up on you. Now he's gone and I miss him terribly.

Omniscient

The Lord knows everything there is to know
We only know what our Lord will allow
When troubled we don't know which way to go
He does and shows us which is best right now

Our Lord knows the past, present, and future
We don't even know the present moment
Often we're confused—often we're unsure
God is always wise and intelligent

Atheists tell God does not exist
Agnostics say we can never know God
Infidels all faith in the Lord resist
Viewing our Lord these ways makes one a clod

The universe has a unique design
All forms of life display God's great genius
Showing by design their Maker divine
Wisdom amazing knowledge tremendous

The Lord knows us both our strengths and weaknesses
He knows our great need for forgiving love
He rescues us from sin and wickedness
He shows us the way to Heaven above

Carl Arthur Schomberg
Ridgecrest, CA

Ode to King George

King George,

it took nearly two hundred and fifty years
but it seems we're finally ready now,
we should have set your throne up high on the bow.
The May Flower, indeed, we could have saved all these years,
to have had a king from the start
would now make things simple and clear.
no more fighting over democracy, it wouldn't exist!
The whites would be whiter, the blacks still slaves.
The Chinese, once the railroads were finished,
we'd claim they're ungodly down to the grave.
The American Indian!
Their spirit still roams the wild frontier,
that leads straight into heaven with no trail of tears.
Make America great again? No!
Let's become the nation God called us to be.
Until we learn to defend, respect, and forgive one another
this land of ours will never be free.

David Catching
Santa Fe, TX

Ocean of Love

In the woods I heard a calling
A weeping willow was franticly balling
No eyes a tearing but a constant flow
So, I followed a stream to see...
Where it would go?

Into the woods among the oaks and pines
Between the bushes and hanging vines...
Strangely enough tears fell into a brook...
Curiosity dared me as I continued to look...

The brook ran into a river shortly running by
Amazing all this water come from crying eyes
I stayed the course didn't want the tears to stray
Soon the river fell magically into a moonlit bay...

The bays tears shimmered by the moonlit sky
As my lids tired, I dare not close my eyes
Slowly the tears merged into a nearby ocean
From this experience I theorized the notion...

We all swim in competition to experience life
Beating out our siblings for her riches surprise
Only to find our happiness and sorrow filled tears
All journey into an ocean of foam...racing towards
Some mystical island of sand where we rest alone...
Waiting for the next wave to appear...memories of home!

Theodore P. Colterelli
Middletown, NJ

Nothing Costs

Nothing costs! If you think I fib, then go to
Walmart, ask one of the cashiers, give me something
In this store for nothing? After her brief chuckle she
Would answer, you can't get nothing in this store with
Nothing, furthermore if you don't leave I'm going to call
The cops then have you arrested for trying to sell this
All-or-nothing estafa. Well if that don't beat nothing,
Then I'm a bear with nothing to do but sit around and
Make nothing out of nothing. I don't care what that big
Mouth cashier says. Nothing from nothing leaves nothing!
I have nothing else to say...nothin! What are you going to do about it?
Just as I expected...nothing! May not look like nothing, yet it
Doesn't mean it's nothing! What was your cost?...Nothing!

Marshall Thompson
Buffalo, NY

I owe my poem and story telling ability to my loving, deceased mother. Oh boy, could she spurn a yarn from the least mundane subjects. I love you, Mom! signed Marshall, The Old Dude.

Never Stop

I'll never stop loving you because you're not here.
I'll never stop caring for you either.
I'll never stop thinking of you.
I'll never stop crying
because I miss you.

I know you're here with me.
I know you can hear me.
I know you can see me.
I will never get used to the fact
that you're gone.
I know sometimes you're here next to me.
I feel that you're near me right now.

I'll never stop crying
because I miss you.
I'll never stop loving you because you're not here.
I'll never stop caring for you either.
I'll never stop thinking of you
because
I miss and love you with all my heart.

Laura M. Keifer
Amsterdam, NY

Moving On

As I sit here and ponder
And try to believe
I start to just wander
Through old memories.

Did I make the right choices
When I picked up my things?
Did I hear the wrong voices
When I tried out my wings?

Now that it's all wrong
I have to reflect,
Did I just follow a song
To cause a big wreck.

I thought in the end
It would turn out to be great.
But since I hit send
It's a great big mistake.

Heidi Marie Kibbe
North Syracuse, NY

My Love

Starry daze
Starry nights
High in the clouds
Searching for my love
Daydreams
Nightmares
Asleep in the clouds
Searching for my love
Mountains high
City streets
Head in the clouds
Searching for my love
Ocean waves
River bends
Rain in the clouds
Pouring down on me
Searching for my love
Nowhere to be found...

Jennifer Ann Lotzer-Smith
Appleton, WI

To My Love on Our Wedding Day

My love, my sweetest love, you came to me at a time that I was weak, broken inside. And like a clock you polished me up and tuned up my parts. You made me run again. You made my heart tick again. You turned me on your favorite station and listened to the sound of my heart beats freely and with purpose so softly. My love, my dearest love, you are the reason I believe in love. That love to me does exist. All of my flaws were spread out for you to see. You looked past them and said I see you for who you are. You taught me something. That growth in love and life is necessary. That we evolve when we must. You taught me to wake up every morning and be nothing less than inspirational, extraordinary. You taught me to know that I am worthy of being loved. I am granted permission to love without boundaries. You taught me that a broken record still plays, that we do not all heal similarly. I am your equal. My heart beats for you. My breath is your breath. From this day until my last, I make one promise to you: to love you passionately, unconditionally, and indefinitely without limits. Today my love, you are loved.

Emauri Danielle Vinson
Norman, OK

My Happy Place

Lovely tree, immediately eye-catching
I claimed you right away
I wander by for frequent glimpses
Some days I provided drops of water
Sun, nurturing
Admirably, you claim me, too
Dependence on each other grows
In exchange for water
You provide food
In exchange for sun
You provide shade
Even without words
We feel each other's love
My hair begins to gray
And you lose your leaves
But beauty is still recognized
Lovely tree, you're still a sight to see
Full of wisdom, wonderful provider
You'll forever be my happy place
For as long as your roots allow you to stand

Kimberli Witucki
San Antonio, TX

My Grandma Korstad

The person now whom I am thinking of
had a kind heart filled with joy and love
Early every morning she'd wake and rise
ready to help me and give me advice
She was in her eighties, wrinkled and old
with a vivid memory of tales untold
Some may be sorrowful and others pleasures
but we didn't know as they were her treasures
After school I'd find her alone upstairs
often reading as she had no cares
She had one failure and that was her sight
but other than that she was very bright
The person I've been telling you about
was my Grandma Korstad without a doubt
She lived with us for many years
and to me she was special and very dear

Becky Stakston
Westby, WI

My Final Decision

I joined the military
And was sent off to war.
I had my perceptions,
But it was so much more.

I couldn't have imagined
The things I would see.
I knew during the fighting,
They'd try to kill me.

When my hitch was over
And I had returned home,
Even if among my friends,
I still felt all alone.

Who could understand all
The carnage I'd seen,
The pain I relived
Every night in my dream?

I just couldn't continue
To live life this way.
Not trusting anyone,
I didn't know what to say.

I had only one thought
Of how to get relief,
But by killing my pain,
I caused my family painful grief.

Neal A. Carl
Endwell, NY

My Dearest Only Sister

I saw Grandma in your face
as you slept with dream unknown
I wanted it to be untrue
the doctors were not right
then I wondered if you knew
if you had already glimpsed "the light"
I wanted it to be over
I wanted it to be fast
I wanted you to linger
I wanted you to be well
I wanted us to start over
With me not being in charge
I thought of Elvis Presley
his "Little Sister" song
you put me on a pedestal
that was always way too high
While you with your quiet strength
your belief in the unknown
Gave up your life grieving
Over a marriage that could not be saved
With your leaving I've felt a little peace
From the drama of your years long illness
But can you tell me "little" sister
Can you tell me how to grieve
When I can't believe my "little shadow"
Will follow me no more

Laura L. Paulsen
St. Paul, MN

My Childhood Dream

I want to leave this one-horse town of broken dreams and empty promises.
My life is no bed of roses, just useless weeds and unmoved grass and dandelions.
Please, get the lawn mower man to cut and trim the untrimmed lawn of wild debris.
There's a holocaust of bitter relationships and helpless romance that went south for the winter like the birds that went to Capistrano.
Just like Dr. Hannibal Lector told young Clarisse—fly, fly, fly!
Who's playing doctor and psychiatrist to whom?
Psychological mind games with Dr. Lector, you don't want to play.
Can you save face with Dr. Lector before he eats your face?
I have to leave my dreaded ghost town of dried tumble weeds and windy dust, like the dustbowl of The Grapes of Wrath.
I'm like William Randolph Hearst, a womanizer, married to ten wives and never satisfied.
Where's my Rosebud, my sled from my innocent childhood?
I whisper, "Rosebud, my poems of yesterday, today, and tomorrow.
I'm a poet and didn't know it.
My immortal verse, call me, Hearst."

Christopher Taylor
Montclair, CA

Your Royal Majesties

Taunted by snowflakes as you slowly bow your petals
Standing against rocks to keep you strong
Seemingly broken and tattered by lives daily stress and
burdens of the flowing icy winds
Beaten down by the winter freeze
Looking as if to be withered and blown away by the
cold winter's storm.
Once again, you stand tall in the glow of spring's sunlight
Donned in violet robes in the radiance of the
early morning sun
Displaying your beauty as a royal court
Somehow knowing others want to adore your
royal majesties
As bees busily graze your eloquent petals
they spread your abounding splendor

Cecilia Hattendorf
Hesperia, CA

Look at the Past

On the farm we had horses that took us places.
The horses would plow our fields, not tractors.
The work was hard but didn't matter.
There was always food on our plate but first
we said grace. Children walked to school where
they learned their manners, had books to read,
and followed up answers. Everyone was happy;
there was love all around and no gossip at all.
There was no such thing as a phone call.

Lu Ann Pederson
Bethel, MN

Most Extraordinary

Ordinary days and lonely nights
Shopping trips and fantasy flights

Friends and family all around
Both feet firmly on the ground

But I needed you to feel complete
And waited for our stars to meet

And then you came one lovely day
And changed my life in your special way

Days and nights once so ordinary
Have now become most extraordinary

Rose Bloom
East Brunswick, NJ

Creatures of Light and Darkness

This faint moon upon the path
Is why fireflies cast their little flash
Where owls hum a distant 'who'
A sleepless toad may burp a little, too
A mother's wing over her young
The caterpillar's fate won't be unsung
Not when the forest is this still
Sleep then during the day he will

Mike P. Kapa
Renton, WA

Moonlight Sonnet

Sitting now in quiet contemplation, alone,
Of that moon we viewed, I reminisce.
Your sweet eyes to mine, your long hair windblown,
Passion's blush and heavy breath, Oh, what a kiss!
We walked in the garden, and gazed up at the stars.
Smiling, as you told me you saw a face on the moon,
A night like this must be meant for a love as ours!
The night grew chilly and it was over too soon.
Ah, forever when, the moon I do see,
But I think of that night, the moon, so bright,
And what would I see, but you, smiling back at me,
Making me less lonesome, my evening light!
  For it is you who brightens my life,
    As you are my lover, my love—my wife!

William R. Foss
Port St. Lucie, FL

Midnight Rising

She was artless,
A philosopher of thought, a sage of reflection,
And he her familiar.

He was contrived,
An aficionado of illusion, a maestro of disguise,
And she his figurine.

She was fairness,
A child of naivety, a wellspring of simplicity,
And he the breaker.

He was deception,
A beast of barbarity, a mercurial bête noir,
And she the hunted.

He, with a hunger for dominance,
Preyed,
And, under veiling humanity betrayed,
Cussed tongue and unhallowed eyes.

She, but a starless chasm starved,
Prayed,
And, against yawning humility shown,
Ashen traces of crooked fiction.

Serenity Morales
San Antonio, TX

Light at the Evening End of Sun

Light at the evening end of sun
Is shot with an intricate, wrinkled rhyme,
Streaming yellow and staining red,
Painting and splashing itself through time.

The mind is huge, burnished and old—
A disc of it slips under the sky.
Embodied by spaces and their worlds,
That sliver of it only seems to die.

Neal Donner
Los Angeles, CA

Metamorphosis

Wrapped in a cocoon
Natural incubation
Metamorphosis...

Delicate creature
Striking wings of symmetry
Buoyant butterfly...

Colorful creature
Flitting among the flowers
Antennae twitching...

Constantly suckling
Taste of a liquor never brewed
Bonny butterfly...

Mary A. Gervin
Albany, GA

Confinement

My mind is confined to the solitude of these four walls
Black and sometimes white the colors the revolve
The ones that are in constant sight
Confined to my own mind is a dangerous hell
Who knows what things my mind might conjure
What demons may dwell
For all is foresaken in this endless well
Sometimes happiness roams
Sometimes spite
Sometimes sadness barges in with all its might
Sometimes anger
Sometimes greed
Until the moment hit when I yell
JUST LET ME BE !
Prisoner of my own mind
Is what I become
I hope to just one day

Get up and run..

Cinthia J. Palma
Corona, NY

My name is Cinthia Palma, born and raised in Queens, NY. Poetry was my outlet for a long time and still continues to be.

Lonesome Chimneys

As I drive by the field, open and wide
the site of the chimney
had me mesmerized!
No home, no fence,
it stood all alone.
Started to imagine
Life! Long ago...
It couldn't be easy
way back then
when ladies were "cooking it all"
and not out of a can.
No washer, no dryer,
or electric, oh my!
They did it all without
a blink of the eye!
I imagine the horse, the buggies,
and wooden picket fences...
the chickens, the rooster,
and good ole Miss Pigpen!
No streetlights, no cars,
a simple guitar,
and a Friday night under the stars!
It only took a minute
to paint a picture in time....
the drive-by and a field
with no one in sight!
But I traveled for a minute
to way back then.
Without leaving the driver's seat
I continued home again.

Corinne Bailey
Huddleston, VA

Loneliness

I never thought I'll be here
I thought I was alone before
But everyone was a distraction
Even if it was for a minute
But now
I have no distractions
I'm completely alone
The loneliness seeps thru
I'm alone and scared
My imagination comes to play
With something that doesn't exist
I have thousands of friends
But I see right thru them
There not real
There not here
I'm trapped
I have no one
I'm completely alone
Completely useless
Forever alone

Stephanie Stoyak
Sandy Hook, CT

Little Bird

Oh, little bird up on the branch,
why do you sing so loud?
I hear you sing your little song.
What is it all about?
Are you singing for the rain
or your partner far away?
Or is it something that you do on a sunny day?
You seem so busy at that little song.
I'd sometimes like to be with you so the
day would not be so long.
So high upon that tree you sit and sing
your little song.
I'd sometimes like to be with you when
everything is wrong.
To fly away for just one day would really
make it right,
and to sing your little song with you
to make everything bright.
Hey, little bird, who do you sing to?
What is the song you sing
up so high in the tree in the sky
with your song so loud and clear.
Hey, little bird, who do you sing to?
Would you sing that song for me?

Neva P. Rootes
Bath, NY

Liability

She's annoying and a drag
You can't take her anywhere
She gets too excited and can't be quiet
She lights up a room which should have stayed dark
Leaves her fingerprints on every little thing

She's a brainiac and has a curious mind
Too much energy and positivity
Nothing much gets her down
A ray of sunshine and a breath of fresh air
She's a liability

I wish she would just tone it down
Give the attention she earns to someone else
How dare anyone say it jealousy
She's a liability
We've all torn her down
So she doesn't see all her amazing qualities

She cries herself to sleep
A dark curtain between who she really is
And who we all tell her she is
She's a liability

Too much potential and admiration
Can't let her know how much we all envy her

She's a liability

Lauren Elizabeth Jordan
Mt Sterling, KY

I am currently a college student at the University of Kentucky studying political science. What inspired me to write this poem were events in my life and people who have been in it. I have been told that I have such great qualities only for people to put me down, which hurt me—only for me to realize it was other people's jealousy and unhappiness with themselves.

Let Go

The desires you have for me have
given a new light on love and intimacy.

An ever-changing flow within me,
a current of never-ending change
that proceeds in amazement.

The thought of giving oneself to
have what each other are in need
of simply astounds me.

Though giving up what is needed
to another is rarely what we do.

Over and over we choose to not
give up what we refuse to surrender.

If only we choose to let go
and begin to let it flow from
within then without will it show the
beauty of the bounty it beholds.

Let go, let God

Lisa Fellers
Hays, KS

Lemon Orchard

Destinations
unknown, unseen.
Time
pending in universal speculation.
Distractions
diverting beyond the horizon of the present,
destined for a florid aura.

A deep breath—
deeper, deeper,
brighter, not darker.

Recollection—

it is not yet afternoon,
only eleven,
as I cruise St. Cloud Boulevard
among a sunshine Heaven.
Eleven seventeen,
my mind, the surround,
all serene.
I admire the lemon orchard
with no thought of the next hour,
as I become present
where life is sweet, not sour.

Austin Ward
Mineral Ridge, OH

Last Curtain Call

I am healthy and whole
Ready to play my role
Living life on a stage
Released from this small cage
Stored up my emotions
Yelled NO to potions
Got to do it my way
I have plenty to say
Can't imagine a flop
Wise to use a stage prop
My words will be flowing
Like rain or white snowing
Basking in the light
Loud applause feels so right
This journey of my life
Filled with chaos and strife
Comes down to right choices
Hushed dissenting voices
Choices are good or bad
Take the good and be glad
When God's destiny calls
No time to shop at malls
Act on His holy will
Pray that you fit the bill
When the curtain comes down
God's face is smile or frown

Inez Jackson
Jacksonville, FL

Keepsakes

Settle shelves of dust,
Hoarders trinkets rust,
One mans junk
Is another ones treasure
Are all these items
For the best of pleasure
Watching things move,
Statues,
A mental,
Emotional issue,
Hard facing facts
All gemstone facets
Hold onto mementos,
The only ones
Keep those,
The rest of them can go,
Cherish what you should hold close
Don't let it go.
If you leave it someday
You'll be coming back for more.

Renee Danes
Bloomingdale, MI

What makes us truly happy in this world? Most stuff doesn't. What we cherish about things are that they were from people who love us as well. Let us clean off our cluttered life and just look like we had enough.

Isabella

At twenty-one weeks this is my first
and last mile

My angel will help me give you
another smile

We tried for twenty-four—breathe into
my unready lungs once more

Your love and kindness forevermore

My stillborn twin, Gabriella, is awaiting
to hear of our strand

What it was like one pound nine ounces
cradled in the palm of your hand

Margaret Coralie Pearce
Englewood, CO

In the Early 1950s

The colder chilled air's early arrival
heightens excitement of seasonal survival
now being on in my years
enveloped with fond memories and tears
holiday spirits reach out to reminisce
Dad's small '52 Chevy convertible
and Mom's engagement fur coat now warming me
Dad put his suit jacket around his wife's shoulders
then the crunch of tire's chains soothing slumber
as holiday spirits reach out to reminisce
Carefully to Dziadek's tree-lined dirt drive he took us
carrying me up second floor wooden steps to ours
in Dziadek's house where we all lived
and now where none of us any longer live
Holiday spirits reach out to anamnesis
The loudness of the sound it awoke me
alone quietly descending as darkness hid me
Dziadek lay on his living room floor pointing
unknown tall man to bait me hovering
as holiday spirits reach out to anamnesis
Being blessed the hospital let me see him
in wool leggings matching coat small before him
where had my white goose-feather tree absconded
restorative thaumaturgy had been remedied
as holiday spirits reach out to reminisce

Marilyn Winter
Toms River, NJ

If I Could Do It All Over Again

If I could do it all over again
yielding my will to Him
surrendering myself to Him
the God of Heaven and Earth

Be thankful for everything
Thankful for the pleasant things of life
and the unpleasant experiences as well
the trials and triumphs
the losses and gains

Not grieving over yesterday's failures
Not worrying about tomorrow's responsibilities
But facing each day as it comes without complaining

If I could do it all over again
not having the mindset of
what the world is capable of doing for me
but what are my capabilities to help myself

Live life to the fullest
Stop living selfishly
but live to help my fellow man the best I can
If I could do it all over again . . .

Malachi Flemming
Miami, FL

I Want Sisters

I want sisters that will stay forever,
I want sisters to make it all better.
I want sisters that will live forever,
I want sisters that I will love forever.

I have sisters to hold my hands if I feel scary and alone.
Sisters who will protect me if I feel threaten in anyway.
I have sisters who love to hear me sing, or tell them one of my stories.
But if I'm filled with so much pain, they'll comfort me 'till the end.

I want sisters that will stay forever,
I want sisters to make it all better.
I want sisters that will live forever,
I want sisters that I will love forever.

Once they told me that we will never leave you,
To see all these moments, there was no need to worry.
And once they told me that we will always love you,
I wouldn't need to know now because it's the truth.

But what if one day they are both gone—would I feel safe again?
Would I feel alone or should I honor them in memory?
So I would sing a song about them or write them in stories?
When I feel so down, just remember them in the good old days.

I have sisters… I have sisters
I have sisters that will live forever… in my heart.

Shay Puls
Whitehall, MI

Hunting Alone

Hunting is not my native language
But I've been searching within myself lately
On the offensive, though not to take advantage
I've ripped off bandages, echoing the pain
To absorb more light in my skin after it would rain
The scarf around my neck's been burning with questions
Attached to me in my trek at a meaningful pace
In this gradual race for answers of contemplation
In these habits of wanting to break away
In my resolve to cater to proactive action
A deadlock of this kind makes it hard to decide
What type of outcome lies on the other side
If there will be truth, or lies in disguise
I haven't always hunted alone, but I am now
At this moment, I am prone to surrender and bow
But that is something that I will never allow
I've entered this cave to decode the hieroglyphics
Holding onto hope in the form of a lantern
Hoping my signal can be seen from Saturn
I made my S.O.S. as an educated guess
Trying to find solutions to my own fed questions
The same ones that have been burning my scarf
That in turn, left me with a branded mark
I may be hunting alone, but I'll never give in
For every moment, I am fulfilled with a promise
As the sunlight pours into my skin.

Julian Alwyn Wilson
Bellmore, NY

Hey, everyone. My name is Julian, and I love poetry, music, and art as a whole. I'm very thankful to Eber & Wein Publishing and Poetry Nation for providing me with this opportunity. In my personal life, I've been going through some tough times, and this poem, "Hunting Alone," is a reflection of those tough times and finding a light through it all. I hope this piece helps to inspire and remind others that there's always a light at the end of every dark tunnel and phase of life. Thank you for reading!

How Well Do You Know Her?

In a simple way, gorgeous drapes her face,
Behind that shadow, she chooses what to hide.
Steel around her heart's shell keeps her safe.
A choice she has made for years of her young life.
The demeanor of a dominating woman,
In the brown of her richly saturated eyes.
Dare you not look too deeply,
For you may be surprised at the response you find.
You may think of her as uncaring at times,
But her heart exudes in the presence of her young.
Alone she treads the path that perfumes itself
It awaits her like no other, before she comes along.
Brave you would be to question her decisions,
Even the walls that surround her long to know these things.
Too long this precious soul has been hiding,
Far away yet only within the closeness of our feet.
Who would I be to love such a girl?
What the hell do I know about her?
Applause comes from within me,
I know her but I don't know her.
Yes, applause, together we stand for I know her well!
Admire I do the women who carry that skill.
Yet, I want the world to see the heart, the beauty,
The strength hidden under a protected steel shell.

Laura Santos
Carpentersville, IL

I wrote this when struggling to understand a woman's ways of putting on a tough mask to the world while on the inside she's so tender, loving, and kind but strong at the same time.

Home Again

Watching the thin
    feathered tracery
      of spring aspens
         shivering in the wind,
I think of how,
      at home,
  the island dogwood
  blankets the ground.
      Stirred by sea breezes,
      the eastern maples
         haunt my mind;
      even as Indian paintbrush
      and bright orange mallow
         dot this parched
         high desert landscape.
Home—a lifetime ago—
    drenched in the foggy
    remembrances of years,
and a deep sadness fills me:
    if ever these wheels
    could make the journey,
    when I'd arrive
         there'd be nobody there.

Judy-Suzanne Sadler
Cortez, CO

Heaven Bound

God be with us in our last days
Help us to do and know what to say

In this world of turmoil and strife
Please be with us as we leave this life

It's so hard when our time does come
Christians are promised and know He's the One

Have we asked for forgiveness for our sins
With God on our side we will win

We are here but for a moment in time
Eternity is forever our spirits to shine

What is important when we part
Is did we believe with all our heart

Marshelle Carberry
Fresno, CA

Hear Me

Screaming in the distance!
Begging, pleading
Hear my cries! Please, just wait!
Leave me be, and alone you disappear
Left drowning in this whirlpool of lies and deception
Each piece breaks, stabbing pain
Chest, arm and stomach
I've let you down. No I let myself down!
The door about fell from its hinges
The very foundation has been shaken, as it turns to ash
I want to reach you
You scream! I'm not talking about this now or never
I sank in the corner, whole body shaking
Wishing you could just feel me now
Saddening, swollen, sheltered deep within
Hidden and left alone, I've been denied
Shock, and on the edge I teeter
These tears are my river, where I am swallowed and no one is aware
Alone I've slept, shivering in fear, just begging for it all to be clear!
Please! Just hear me now.

Emberly Rose Weaver
Highland Heights, KY

Grandma and I

I have so many great memories of my grandma
who passed away so many years ago.
I still have the blues when her anniversary comes around.
You see, my grandma and I were so close.
One great memory that I treasure the most was
I never knew how to say the rosary.
My grandma said, "Sit down next to me and repeat after me."
That was our most precious time together.
Grandma had an extra rosary and she smiled as she gave it to me.
She knew blue was my favorite color.
She had her crystal rosary in her hands and it sparkled like the stars.
When Grandma was ready to pray she would fold her hands.
That was a sign to me to see if I was ready to say the rosary.
I looked up at Grandma while smiling back at her.
Now that my grandma is gone, I just have so many fond memories of her.
I grab my blue rosary every night before I go to bed.
I would sit down in my favorite chair where my grandma used to sit.
I thought I had the most special rosary ever.
I hold my rosary so proudly for I knew my grandma was with me.
My grandma and I had a great connection and a very spiritual one, too.
This poem is for you, Grandma.
With much love,
Your granddaughter
Pauline Byrnes

Pauline Byrnes
Mineral Point, WI

Gems of Life

Children are precious gems;
Some are emerald, some are diamonds or rubies.
My three gifts from God
Mean everything to me.

The first time I saw their sweet face
Was the greatest moment in my life.
Every time I think of them
Their hearts I forever embrace.

It makes my heart glow with pride
To see how they have grown.
I love them with all my heart
And will forever be by their side.

In my life, they are the best part—
To get to watch them grow
From infants to mature adults.
I love them more than they will ever know.

Rich Ashker
Niagara Falls, NY

Friend

I met an old friend the other day
I don't know from where he came
We both called each other "buddy"
Because we forgot each others names
We talked about birds and trees
And the daffodils that were growing
And about the change in weather
And where the world was going
Money made us laugh
Politics we disregarded
As well as topics from our youth
That wisdom had long bombarded
He stopped laughing after a while
He looked around each way
His eyes wanted to leave
I begged that he please stay
But he huddled up in his coat
Grinned at me warm and kind
Then walked away and disappeared
Into the corners of my mind.

Gabrielle Katerina Blake
Titusville, FL

Our minds are much more interesting than the people we wish would think like us.

Forbidden Love

You walked into my life and stole my heart
Those blue eyes got me at the start.
In my weakest time you came along
and took me where I had not been for so long.
Oh such bliss as this, I can't explain except I am lost in your love.
You are the calm and the storm before the rain that comes from above.
The touch of your lips is like a gentle breeze,
so soft and gentle like a song playing in the leaves.
My heart has been touched like the strings of a violin
Oh what beautiful music to just begin
and I know this forbidden love will one day end.
It's played our song at different times,
like an angel playing beautiful music on the chimes.
The song plays no more and it is quiet,
but there are times I remember it at night.
As sure as the stars shine above,
I will always remember the forbidden love.
Life has a funny way of making things right
even if some think it is wrong.
It may be over but the memories last
and they are very, very strong.

Jerry T. Freeman
Lake City, AR

For You

I'm going to miss seeing
Your cocoa butter skin
With your baby doll brown eyes
Glowing like a full moon.
I'm going to miss seeing
Your small moist pink lips
And your shapely hips.
And I'm going to miss
The thought of hoping
To see you again.

Jessie Epps
Whitmire, SC

Fair Winds and Following Seas

Sail away my dear friend to familiar places where life was sweet
and all the precious memories were made
Let the wind carry you to distant lands where you will be welcomed
and embraced
As you embark on this journey you will never be too far away
I will hear your laughter in the gentle breeze
See the twinkle of your eyes in the distant stars
And feel the warmth of your smile in the rays of the sun
I unlock a chamber in my heart where you will dwell forever

Angelica Hotti
Foster City, CA

I found a photo of a dear friend who passed away recently. In the photo, he and I are on a sail boat, smiling, with the sun on our faces. The photo inspired me to write the poem.

Fire

You stand with your thick bark wild vines well-rooted.
Lofty forceful prideful a testimony of time.
A magnificent stance is ours to behold.
Who's left the open flame, its heart yearning more.
Its gasps for fresh air without stretching hot arms.
Grows quickly spewing out thick black breath into sky.
Moving quickly across the forest floor.
Roaring... its whipping hot tongue on every living thing.
LOUD ROARS...of pleasure it screams out.
Hungry it feeds and feeds devouring.
Your strong thick shell it torches without warning.
Unable run to run, you never saw it coming.
Wrapping over your lofty arms.
The sizzle the crackle the pain...
As it strips you of your pride.
The hot torching flame turns Earth's green to black
Breaking you down till you can't breathe.
In the veil of gray it seems you die.
The calm quiet morning into the leftover haze
What's this I see in blackened soot of forgotten dreams.
A tinge of green
A sprout forgotten by hell's fire
Pushing up where you stood.
I knew you weren't gone—
Not ever gone for good.

Char Marie Cook
Tallmadge, OH

Empty

Empty hallway—no more pictures,
no more reflections of memories and moments.
Empty ball jar, sitting on the counter, glaring at me,
wondering why I never learned how to can.
How many times I sat in the house
upon the faded blue couch or the worn green one.
There I'd spend the years after I grew out
of the toy horses and cows, Barrel of Monkeys and Lincoln Logs,
never quite connecting with the souls around me.
I stare at the last full jar;
carefully-sliced tomatoes still drifting
in their ruby juices with amber seeds.
It's a beautiful mess.
The jar is sealed tightly—
feelings and tomatoes sealed up perfectly.
A few quick turns, my throat tightening as the lid loosens.
The lid pops off; my lips and eyelids clench to ward off the tears.
I lift the jar and tip it,
watching the crimson chunks glide
towards the opening and slip and plop into the pot.
I stare at them for a few minutes.
Her loss means those long-ago memories are the last,
those canned tomatoes were the last,
no more new can be made.
The jar is empty now,
like the hallways, the rooms, the house once a home.

Sarah Elizabeth
Rapid City, SD

In June of 2014, my grandfather passed away. Six months later, his wife, my grandmother, died instantly in a car crash. As a child, whenever my family would go to their house, she always had a jar full of cookies, as well as jars of homemade pickles and other goods from her garden. She made the best green bean casserole—the only way I'd willingly eat green beans as a child. As we cleaned up the house after she passed away, we found the stores of her recently canned produce and amongst these, the above-mentioned tomatoes.

Do You Remember?

Do you remember as a child the
first time you saw spring?
The tulips and the daffodils
the sunshine and the rain?
The walks along a country road
the visit to the park?
The daisies in a field of green,
a singing meadowlark?
Do you remember summertime—
those warm and temperate days—
when you played pretend in the yard
a hundred different ways?
And then there were the camping trips,
the fishing, and the hikes;
The hotdogs and the ice cream cones,
the wagons and the bikes.
Do you remember as a child your
playmates fond and dear?
Your buddies, pals, and special friends
who changed from year to year?
Do you remember growing old
and what a part age played?
And looking back you realize
those were the golden days.

Larry Sabiston
Worthington, IN

Divinity Is Life, Life Is Love

it all starts with a spark of the soul
the breath and heartbeat is our home
in human nature we are never alone
we are beings of habit flowing in cycles
creating our realities confined in shackles
with fears and shadows hiding our true self
mindlessly engaged in a chase for wealth
hate and ignorance our society creates
letting the past go is not up for debate
following our light will lead to balance
building this habit will take practice
yoga and meditation is a friend to any
learning from life itself will be canny
to be anything we believe we can be
reframing our thoughts is all we need
for us to plant our manifestation seed
nothing will matter more than empathy
when embracing a journey to harmony
our energy chakras will glow in alignment
together we shape universal enshrinement
guiding our youth with examples of love
innermost peace initiating our rise above
growing as one we will wear our crown
realizing all that we have is right now
nature is our teacher and imagination is key
to conquering our minds for us to be free

Lorenzo Cordero Bennett
Bronx, NY

Deceit

Oh! What tangled webs we weave
When we first practice to deceive.
Whether lying, cheating, trickery, fraud,
In this practice nothing is odd.
We twist those words and make them sound
Like they've been laid on solid ground.
Then we start to plot our scam
To put another in a jam.
When all is done we feel so proud
And want to shout it all out loud.
Blindly thinking all is bright
When we feel the job's done right.
But remember—
Whatever falses your disguise
The wool's pulled over your own eyes.

Teresa Clanton
Kingston, TN

What a Woman

What a woman you are
A gem so rare
The strength of a tower
On target every hour
And a pleasure to be near.
Are there many like you
Who can undertake tasks
And see them to the end?
Let me send an e-mail
Make sure you are there
As you are now woman of the year.

Bernice Chandler
Queens, NY

Death Awaits

Just over your left shoulder
Death lives
Silently in mid-air she awaits a landing.

Maybe she will cruise in
Like a smooth surfer on a crunching ocean wave.
Or perhaps she will land smack on your windshield
Like a disoriented bug.
Then again death might come softly on cat paws
During a dark and starry night.

Just over the left shoulder
Death lives.
Be you minutes old upon this earth or a century plus
She awaits a landing
Upon your heart and soul.

Will you embrace her?
Will you scorn her?
Will you laugh at her?

Whatever your hospitality to death
She continues to wait
Perched in mid-air
Just over your left shoulder.

Phyllis Tyler
El Monte, CA

Cucamonga Sunrise

In the fading darkness
Faint stars linger
The sun a rose-colored whisper
Beauty and wonder unfolding
Like petals on a flower

Steadily the sun rises
In a blaze of glory
Creation breathing a soft hymn
Of God's sweet love
Into my hungry heart and soul

Along a wooded path
The flutter of falling leaves
Alive with brilliant colors
Soar freely
On pine scented breezes

Bathed in the splendor of sunrise
Wispy clouds cling
To snow dusted peaks
Birds winging graceful silhouettes
Against the sun's fiery colors

In the crisp morning sweetness
The lazy sleepy silence
Echoes with the soft call
Of a mourning dove
Haunting and beautiful

Rebecca Burns
Rancho Cucamonga, CA

Comrades

I am one of the many sent
to foreign and distant lands
There we fight against oppression
with weapons, our hearts, our hands

I see or hear no difference
to me, their cultures are unknown
The man who stands beside me
Is my faith that I'm not alone

Night is our friend and protector
it's not easy to face the day
In our hard-won moments of quiet
we bond, we hope, and we pray

Lost some of our best today
won't leave our own in lonely places
You'd know we are all comrades
by the tear tracks on our faces

Some days our gods favor us
we are powerful and holy blessed
Mile after mile after mile we march
not once do we falter or rest

Each mile is our flag to freedom
we seek not our glory or fame
If I should fall and never rise
my comrades will remember my name

Carole A. Stewart
Lompoc, CA

Closet

It started half past midnight, in utter silence
It was so silent you could not hear the screaming rain
That's when the creaking of my bedroom closet lead
to an appearance that did not feel human
So, I did what all growing girls should: sank into the depths
of my psychosis
Used one hand to smother my vagina for fear of this uncontrollable
hysteria and used the other to promptly strangle Mr. Roosevelt
I sweat and shake through this potential rape, homicide
which for some reason is still a cultural phenomenon
Still my insides were in an internal battle
as his footsteps slowly began to approach my bed
Oh no I peaked, which elongated into a stare
And his stillness gave me very questionable thoughts
I jumped at the thump; wait is he on his knees?
He started begging for mercy
declaring that he and his lover had quarreled hours before
and he was devastated by the whole ordeal, he could barely
breathe
And through this devastation, he lost all track of time, which
lead us to our current situation
Please pause a moment I too need to check my breathing
Lights on, he rose like an angel and I saw his light gray fur
through his copycat Skellington suit
and between his ears laid Mr. Mudgett's boulder cap
He used his snow-white paw as an opposable thumb to place
it over where the human heart lays and held his head in shame
He apologized for the inconvenience and what he did next
could only be defined as remarkable

Shaunna M. Ingrassia
Holbrook, NY

City Girl Against the World

She sits under the scaffolding with bright lights on her face.
Her back holding up the building, her knees holding up her spine,
and her sign holding up the world.
Brown hair curls out of a bun, as limp as the hands curled in her lap,
And she is silent.
I stop and watch,
    As everybody passes her by without a dime to spare.
Why is she nobody's main concern?
I am in awe of this city girl, holding up the world with her pain.
My last $8, saved towards the clothes I cannot afford
    Seem like millions when I think of her nothingness,
And I know in my heart as I fill up her cup
That these bills must seem like the world
To this desperate city girl.

Hazel Lynn McCulla
Richmond, VA

What inspired me to write this poem was a trip up to New York City. My family has been middle class my entire life. With my mom working for the government and my dad owning his own business, we've always been comfortable. We took a trip to New York City and I saw a homeless girl, who wasn't much older than me, on 5th Avenue just sitting very resigned on a street corner. I gave her my last $8 and I just hope that made a difference to her that day. It just really struck a cord with me how similar we were in age and how easily I could end up like that someday.

Choice

When you have to make a moral choice,
think about the subsequent consequences,
because going along with other misguided
individuals can lead to unintended results.

When you think of coveting something,
ponder the grief it could bring to others
who really treasure and use the article,
and would need vitality to replace it.

When you have a chance to help others,
lend a hand with grace and cooperation.
Some day you too may need assistance.
The benefits of selflessness are evident.

The choices appear when not expected.
Electing a self-fulfilling path is easy to do,
but morals tell us, it's better to help others
and inspire a positive agenda for humanity.

When you have a chance for personal gain,
that will unnecessarily destroy some other,
pause and consider; is this the right thing?
Is this a good example for others to follow?

Gordon Bangert
Vail, AZ

Change

Some like change
Some do not.
Changes come
Ready or not.

Changes appear
All day long.
Some are pleasant
Some are all wrong.

Be flexible my friend;
Changes come unaware.
Some make us falter
Some make us care.

But I've found One who
Can help us through it all—
God! His Holy Spirit
Is the winner over all.

Don't fret about change
When it's out of our hands
Why we'll even be changed
When He gives the command "Change."

Betty L. King
Knoxville, TN

Lost

The stagnant odor of lost
Filled the cold winter day
Like a kettle on the stove
Curling steam upwards. Stays.
Lost permeates, encamps.
The chill inhabits the soul
And lays to waste the vast
Pages of the heart's boehl.
The giant black shadow
Leaps up to devour me,
Tying my uttermost thoughts
With a twisted rope, tightly.
Lost is a cold, dark night
Suffocating, storm tossed,
Blocking out the light
With the stale odor of lost.

Ruth Marie Mann
Forest, MS

Cadence of Ivory

I hear the whispers of the crowd behind the curtains
They threaten to tear my walls down
Just breathe, I tell myself, deep breaths
My heart is pumping blood to my limbs
I can feel it flowing through me
My heart is beating a torrent against my chest
I take another deep breath, the time has come
I take the stage, head held high
Outside I look poised and confident
But inside the walls are crumbling
The piano sits in the middle of the stage, it is grand
I sit at the bench and wonder who sat there before me
Did the nerves still their hands?
Perhaps they played without a care in the world
I fight the nerves back
I try to control the ache that's eating at me
Focus, I tell myself, and just breathe
My hands are itching to play, for the time has come
My fingers press the ivory keys down
It is a melody only I know, written by my own mind
My fingers remember the rhythm of the harmony
The music is my soul, its pattern beats with my heart
There is where I belong—a cadence of ivory

Brittany Sarkozi
New Boston, MI

By Your Side

Happiness is the new rich
Health is the new wealth
Friendship is the new love
Inner peace is the new success

My patience is the new understanding
That when you grow, change and balance
You are ready for your new life

In the moments of needing space
I am always favoring you
And hope you receive my grace

You are a worthy man
Lord knows you must fulfill your plans
To be true to who you are

Know that from any sky
I am wishing you the best of my
Birthday wishes coming true

This last line is now meant for you

Heather Petrina
Mount Kisco, NY

By My Window

One day, I sat by my window
and gazed out over my yard.
For what I saw there,
I began to laugh real hard!

The neighbors grass was growing
so much faster than mine.
He'll soon have to mow again,
and to me that will be just fine!

Then I looked down to the corner
just as far as I could see.
They were busy spreading fertilizer
while I got mine for free!

Now it really doesn't matter
what all those neighbors think.
While they are busy watering,
the rain gives mine a drink!

I'll tell you where there's magic
and where the wind does blow.
My leaves fly to the neighbors;
I know they love me so!

Enola J. Steinbach
Waupaca, WI

Bluebirds and Blackbirds

They fly by day, rest by night. Can they fly solo or together?
When they rest, how many to a nest?
When they sleep, do they dream bright or simply weep?
When they eat, how much intake until their bellies are full?
When they fly, do their wings soar high enough to answer
each other's call?
For they are the magical bluebirds, the birds that often make
skies shine brighter.
They can make sullen days more amiable; they make dark
moments seem tolerable.
Which birds fly higher, which birds are more fierce, which
birds seem to be more stoic?
Is it the blue jay, blue bunting, painted bunting, or indigo bunting?
Or perhaps the Florida scrub-jay, western scrub-jay, Bahama swallow,
tree swallow, cerulean warbler, or black-throated blue warbler?
A short while back I noticed a few flying high freely up into
the blue day. I sat and pondered, how long must they fly
before they decide to rest and lay?
Is it conceivable they are perhaps being hunted by a larger bird, one
stalking their prey? Not a songbird. Not a bluebird. Maybe a blackbird?
This adversary could be mightier, more ferocious. Will it eat
up the bluebird? Will it swallow and swoop, swallow and swoop?
Had this beast swallowed and swooped faster or harder?
Might it have pierced, serrated, baited? Might it have surmised
and diced, clipped and nipped, fight while in flight with no end in sight?
One with teeth that will crunch and maim, crunch and maim, inflicting
great pain?
Will it leave its opponent aloof while keeping its kin in or out of the loop?
Might this larger bird devour the humble bluebird? Might it swallow and
swoop, swallow and swoop, swallow and swoop?

Jake Wasinger
St. Charles, IL

Bloom Where You Are Planted

The winter wind squalls and nothing lingers,
as it sends restless leaves scurrying past!
Trees stand scolding, with pointed fingers
gnarled with age, yet still steadfast.
Soon the whiteness of the snow
will blanket memories of all the roses,
and spring will wait, snuggled in,
all except the holly bough's red noses!

Robbie Tynes
Ardmore, OK

Blackballed

Have you ever been blackballed?
Do you know what it means?
To be rejected, an outcast, belittled and demeaned.
The word blackballed is no laughing matter.
It is time when you experience libel and slander.
So, before you blackball someone always know this.
What goes around comes back around, in just a matter of
time you reap what you sow, this you should know.
Therefore, whether you or someone you know is blackballed,
pray to God it does not happen to you.
I believe if you were blackballed you would not know what to do.
Believe me, being blackballed is alive and true.
If it were not for God's Grace keeping me alive, being
Blackballed is impossible to survive.

Esther Grace Simmons
Savannah, GA

Black Minds in the Wind

Whirling thoughts of our forever waving conscience.
Consumed within a vacuum of dark opposition.
Whistling through tribulations we forever wave amongst the stars,
to light the days.
Rejected, shunned, and claiming us as rotted fruits.
Forever we wave a sustainable root.
Look beyond the tree and see.
There is a form like the firstborn, invisible yet it transcends.
Here is where the mind exists.
The place is called every place and no clouded perception will ever
begin, that faithful ride amongst this wind.
A free-blowing wind, free from assimilation and true to form.
We live, we die, we live again Black Minds in the Wind.

Stanley Robert Dorsey
Washington, DC

I wrote this poem in appreciation of all the things that black people tried to accomplish for the betterment of all and failed.

Beware of the Mole

There's a mole in the hole driving me mad,
So I purchased a trap, the best I've had.
These varmints destroy landscape faster than anything might do,
But, one snap of this trap, their day is through.
The moles have tunnels starting deep in the ground,
Just open one up their expressway is found.
They move through the earth with great ease,
Making a mess wherever they please.
These pests search for worms, grubs and larvae on which to dine,
While leaving the look of a war zone behind.
The first time one of these creatures invades your space,
You'd swear ten were working at a feverish pace.
As I exercise each morning walking our block,
I notice the moles have worked 'round the clock.
Creating more tunnels leaving mounds of dirt piled high,
Hope they're caught before they multiply.
So get out in your yard and find the mole run,
Set a trap and wait for the spring to be sprung.
Once the mole is hungry and on the move,
Your chance to nab one definitely improves.

William P. Bessler
Cincinnati, OH

Beauty

Can be described in many ways and facets; however, beauty to me, only as I can foresee, has brought me to this moment of intimate poetry.
Beauty has the contents of being beautiful inside and out.
Perhaps it's the heavenly stars standing against the deep black skies while flying about.
Even the autumn trees are gorgeous gleaming in the brilliant sun; as if God painted them with His fingertips.
"I am the Alpha and the Omega," says the Lord God, "the One who is, who was, and who is coming, the Almighty," divinely speaking these words from His lips.
Perhaps the beauty of the courageous, black stallion "Black Beauty," of movies seen, with his coat brushed slick and shining like one in a million.
Even the sleek doberman pincher in a coat of black is most stunning as the soft, gentle black rabbit, the spotted Ocelot, and the mysterious Siamese jet black cat.
Cherished is the beautiful "Mr. Lincoln" with big petals of deep red like a red velvet rose or the Barbara Bush, salmon pink, a stunning rose and so is the mystic purple black rose.
But it's the simple, fabulous black orchid I've chosen.
Black is beautiful says the cliché; show me the tall, well-built, intellectual, fine black man, Italian, or white.
And I will say? Ya! But: The man of pure beauty, inner peace, strength of grace, loving, and all-knowing said, "I am the Rose of Sharon and the Lily of the Valley." Our Lord is bountiful.

Ethelyn Barnes
Kansas City, MO

I Love You, Marion

I love you, Marion
My heart is an open soul
I love you, Marion
There's no sound in my music
Lonely is the night without you
I love you, Marion
I won't be the same without you
I love you, Marion
My heart is an open soul
I love you, Marion
You're more than the summer sun
I love you, Marion

Jack Camp
Boston, MA

Bad Company

Bitter taste in my mouth
After a delicious meal
Perfectly seasoned
But with the wrong accompaniment
One note gone awry
Infusing the whole experience
Leaving behind a sourness that a lemon would envy
Burning it's way down my esophagus
The acidic juice consuming my heart
Waking me in the middle of the night
And haunting me like a sun dried tomato
Irritating my insides and causing my thoughts
to whirl like a salad spinner.

Sonia Cardwell
Salinas, CA

This poem was inspired by the energy that you sometimes absorb when you share time with company and everything goes well except you are left feeling robbed of joy.

As the Wind Blows

From whence does it come and where does it go
that current sweeping tinder—seasons' molting undertow?

In play, ethereal fingers gently pluck loosened leaves,
puppeteering dances, looming flora in the weave.

Caressing, taunting, tickling, and coaxing,
nipping, spraying, teasing, and hoaxing;
frolicking in jest,
alchemist at best!

In a frenzied rage it's malevolent force,
levels willful destruction without remorse!

Sculpting each storm till it's peaceful descent;
eagles suspended till the mysteries are spent.

Shearing, splicing, twisting, and tearing,
heaving, razing, wrecking, and killing;
aerial predator in flight,
calamity in sight!

This pilgrim's impulse delights in surprise;
its direction and flare—none can surmise.

Whispers or wails,
the wind carries a tale!

Susan Elizabeth Liebl
Franklin, WI

Annie Lesko Left the Lights on at the Farm

Annie Lesko left the lights on at the farm.
She was alone.
Each light became her comfort,
Her protection through the night.

Most passersby would ask with momentary curiosity:
"Who lives there in that broken place
Where fences bend to left and right,
Protecting nothing in their space?"

Annie Lesko watched through windows,
Every curtain pulled aside.
She waited for another day and night to end.
Her life was bound by memories, not friends.

Annie Lesko left the lights on at the farm.
She was alone.

Rita Greco
New Kensington, PA

Annie Lesko once lived in the house across the field from ours. The aroma of sauerkraut often filled the entryway. She always wore a long-skirted dress with a half-apron. When chickens chased me around the yard, she laughed, revealing a "winking" gold tooth. The lonely woman here is not the Annie I knew. I simply used her name and described her house where glowing lights dotted every window throughout the night. I do wish she still lived in the house across the field. Instead, she's gone to a better place.

Always Be Humble and Kind

I have a dear friend of mine
who is happy and jolly, just my kind.
Shared God's peace with the shake of a hand,
uplifting spirits were just grand.

Her beautiful voice leads us in song,
putting a smile on my lips where it belongs.
You can just feel that she loves to sing.
Many warm feelings to me it brings.

Taps her foot, keeping up with the beat,
soon will direct us to take our seat.
Let's sing "Always Be Humble and Kind."
These special words make a home in my mind.

Enter my heart and there you will find
these guiding words "be humble and kind."
By now you are picturing Pastor Cindy
whom we will see soon, next Sunday!

Marlene Neubauer
Glidden, IA

All Deserve Recognition

Tragic events and natural disasters
Are remembered for years ever after.
Hurricanes, floods, and wild fires,
Loss of lives and desolate survivors,
Widespread destruction and devastation
Will long be topics of conversation.

So many deserve well-earned recognition.
Responders rush in without hesitation.
Firemen, policemen, EMTs,
And medical staff work tirelessly.
Security teams show bravery
To help with every catastrophe.

Volunteers reach out extending hands,
Donating blood and fulfilling demands.
Monetary aid through contributions
Continue to increase in financial institutions.
Reporters spend hours collecting information,
Spreading it widely through mass communication.

Through every country the news expands.
Prayers echo throughout the lands
For God to hold victims in His hand.
Hearts are saddened, eyes filled with tears,
Brotherly love is displayed to the despaired.
Applause is due all for compassion and care.

Judy Thornton
Leavenworth, KS

Alcohol

Alcohol, the affect you have
On people's lives is so mean
You make me so mad,
I want to scream

You take away the life of some
Mother's precious child
And she will never again on this earth
See that child's beautiful smile

A Father spends so much money
On his desire for you
That he can't feed his family
And to the reason why
He has not a clue

Because of you there are good
People who lose their license
And often go to jail
Spending thirty days or more
Enclosed in an unfriendly locked cell

Of course, I know you will respond
To this by saying, "You see
It wouldn't be a problem if
You didn't drink so much of me"

"If you love me so much that you
Can't get enough of me
You need to get yourself some help
And to that I think we will agree."

Carolyn Councilman
Graham, NC

Agony

My sadness turned to pain
And pain brought a pouring rain
Of anger and despair
That turned to lack of care
Hatred like an epidemic plagued my heart
And all of my securities were torn apart
And the walls were built for protection
Losing all connection
From the outside noise
Was a choice
I made to keep my peace
And let the anger cease
So I can feel my soul
Reviving it was my goal
And in the solitude I discovered
Insight – fully uncovered
That tore away my pride
And let Love reside

Anush Djaniants
3118 Mannington Drive, NC

Adjusting to Change

Life is a series of changes as daughters or sons
from the first day here on Earth
beginning with those diaper ones
that start at time of birth.

We crawl before we walk
and find our way about.
Then we laugh before we talk;
joy, we couldn't manage without.

So now we're growing right along
and learn to be with others.
Next we learn to sing a song
and share our "wants" and "bothers."

The years go by and all too soon;
we're heading to a real big school.
And then begins our chance to bloom
from one grade to another by rule.

The world opens up bit by bit
and then it's graduation time.
How shall we be a hit?
What path shall we define?

The boundaries set only by goals,
so set your mind to achieve.
The range is from pole to pole
Believe! Believe! Believe!

Elizabeth Anne Stuart
Stow, OH

A Weekend Adventure

With our friends Suzanne and Herb
We traveled one sunny day
To Mason City, IA, a busy, lovely burg
A three and a half hour drive away.

It takes all day or more if you can
To see Meredith Wilson, the Music Man.
His Museum Square, his childhood home
And his seventy-six trombones.

We learned so much more than we ever knew
Of his life and talents we had not a clue.
By the end of the day it was our mission
To have ice cream from his Candy Kitchen.

"To the Historic Park Inn" we yell.
Our rooms await at Frank Lloyd Wright's hotel.
We ate and rested really quite well
Until the fire alarm lights and bell!

Confused and disoriented we met in the hall
Except for Herb who sleeps 'au naturale.'
Declared he'd rather "burn in bed"—
That's what he said!

The early morning wake-up call
Was not what John had in mind at all.
Thankful that it was a mistake,
We met at 1910 Grill for eggs and pancakes.

Barbara Crede
Moline, IL

A Toast to the Invisible

What do you say to the invisible?
How do you toast to the one you long to see?
The words that just won't make a difference,
how do you make them count?
Here's to you, some drinks you would have loved.
Your smile one wants to imagine as we
celebrate another anniversary
of the date you claimed
your new life
for
eternity.

Frances Saiz
Santa Fe, NM

I Believe

Today is a new day that the Lord has made
He is such a rock that is also a great shade
He is strong and His hand keep me so safe
He is wise and different with His own pace
I don't know what my next steps will be
But if I am with Christ, He is also in me
I was selfish within once upon a time
But God can change things on a dime
I love my Lord God, Father, Abba, and King
I adore Him and that is why I gladly sing
Oh how great Thou art, so high above all
I smile for He hears me when I humbly call

Debra Kay Johnson
Dayton, TN

A Light Dimmed

It was a bright morning they each had known;
both sleeping in the silence of the night
with their own deepest dreams before waking.

The neighing of the horses at dawn were
wont to be fed as on any normal day,
and the bluish haze of the surrounding
mountains enveloped the fragrant pastures
while singing birds waked all sleeping creatures.

Singing birds did not wake him who slept the
sleep of one who had left the verdant
and fragrant pastures familiar to them,
one who shared bright mornings and warm evenings
with her on each and every single day.
Theirs was a life filled with simple pleasures
as known to them before his light was dimmed.

Irma H. Collins
Winchester, VA

A Great Noise

Lonely People
In hunger, pain, and sorrow
Climb mountains now in storms
Darkness gathers everywhere
And the comfort of God is waiting to be felt
Thousands shout and cry from their very soul
There are no single words
A differing utterance comes from each
A great, but beautiful noise
Now mixed with thunder,
Heard by angels, I do hope
And understood

David M. Schmidt
Panama City, FL

A Glorious Day

Flowers are blooming…
So many beautiful colors to behold
Butterflies, hummingbirds, and bees are all surrounding me
As I stand to admire what nature brings
The clear blue sky is brightened by the sun
It hugs me with its warmth
I see a glorious day that will get me on my way
Walking under the trees brings shade
and a cooling peacefulness
The birds above me are feeding their chicks
They sing with joy I am rejoicing with them
Singing within to the simple pleasures in life that nature brings

Sheryn Scarborough
Seal Beach, CA

A Glimmer of Light

I remember the twirl of the turnstile before the crowd's cheer announced the first pitch.
I remember the flutter of cream curtains when you left mother by the door.
I remember your whiskey-stained breath, while you coerced my innocence.
I remember the flex of your pale ankle before the tension of your first plié.
I remember the furrow splitting your back turned from my opened palm.
I remember the sweat on your upper lip as the charred roof fell on our childhood home.
I remember the vinegar taste in my nose smote by the boulder destined for you.
I remember the kiss of the blood sky blessing our rain-soaked wheat.
I remember your hysterical eyes spitting into my wanting cup.
I remember the twitch of your nose at the command of "I love her."
I remember the turn of your thumb when you sentenced me, eternally.
I remember the flurry of wind-whipped leaves, waving after the departing plane.
I remember the base of your taut spine, coiled round the blasted mortar shell.
I remember you waving the banner, even as my warrior's face was porcupined by arrows.
I remember the hunched back of the busboy, scurrying for our last ship across town.
I remember the crack of the armada's bark sunk behind a soupy mask at dawn.
I remember the stain on the concrete that could never be cleaned.
I remember the phone call you promised that never came.
I remember it all, but I prefer to forgive.

Sean C. Stone
Santa Monica, CA

As a student of history, reflecting on the cruelty and suffering of humans throughout time, I wanted to convey a few moments that could be described as 'universal experiences,' whether we feel we lived through them in past lives, or have felt them as simile to instances in our own present. But despite the darkness, there is always a 'glimmer of light' as the title suggests, for I find myself, at heart, an optimist.

A Gentle Restoration

When differences arrive
and tensions pull us so,
when things are less than hoped for,
we feel the undertow.

Perhaps it's only a moment,
perhaps an hour or two,
you see what I don't see;
your view is not my view.

Yet thoughts are not our words;
restrained, our lips we seal.
Love always holds us steady;
faith keeps us even keel.

And yet it seems a joy
when waves so tall seem small,
when tension ebbs away,
and we, at shore, both see
a gentler, brighter day.

Kenneth Swan
Marion, IN

A Fireman's Farewell

Today a special person was laid to rest.
The sun shone and all his family, friends and co-workers came to pay a very special tribute to one we all loved.
For 40 years he was there to help.
Keeping all the trucks in good shape and giving his best.
He loved life and was there to help anyone in need.
Visiting was pure joy throughout his life.
He was kind and thoughtful and dearly loved his wife.
He served in the war to protect his country.
He was a man of God and served him well.
He was honored today by a service I shall never forget.
Carried to his final resting place on a fire truck he loved.
God has given us a man we all were proud to know, as he touched our lives in so many ways.
The sun shone.
The bugle played and the sound of a 21-gun salute was heard.
Farewell to a loyal servant of God, his family, friends and co-workers.

Roberta E. Drebes
Quincy, IL

What Did You Say, What Did You Mean?

Too many words lay flat on the page
Punctuation does not elevate the feeling correctly
The interpretation becomes multiple choice
Choice one can read angry and critical
Choice two reads outspoken and telling it like it is
Choice three is nonreactive with pondering
The conversation becomes what you make of it
Personal emotion creates a mindset
The input is first person when words are on paper
Your reaction decides emotions delivered
Kind or loving terms can become empty and meaningless
Mean or unpleasant words can jump off the page at you
Even when words are spoken-memory can misplace intent
I am left with-what did you say and what did you mean
The conversation will get a reboot or a dismissal

Christine M. Leckbee
Odessa, TX

We Stand Together

We woke up one day and all was fine
The sun was shining
The radio played happy tunes
Some went to work, others to school
Others went shopping, and some were at home.
The planes flew in the skies
Buses traveled here and there
All was good and all was well....
Until
Our lives were changed by an act of hate
So horrific and devastating
We were all in shock
The towers were struck and fell to the ground
Our Pentagon ruined
Our lives turned upside down
The skies fell deadly silent and the news traveled quickly
Our troops were alerted
The rescuers went to work
Some lives were saved, still many are missing
Under the rubbish and ruin are loved ones and friends
We have seen hell on Earth in our own country this time
We are mourning and sad
We are angry and confused
But through all this destruction
We stand together as one
A country with faith and trust that justice will prevail
We are here to fight—we are here to stay
We are the United States of America!

Sandi Litschewski
Spearfish, SD

Trees in Winter

Autumn leaves are falling down
In colors of yellow, red, and brown.
Tree-limb fingers dancing in the breeze,
Shuddering... thinking sadly of a future freeze.
Leafless, somber trees looking so forlorn—
How many months will go by before they are reborn?
Standing naked with arms stretching up to the sky...
Coolness—becoming colder—haziness... ugh! They sigh.
Trees just don't seem to look so pretty this time of year—
Frost, penetrating cold—this is what they fear.
Majestic, stalwart, and strong...
Birds on branches give lively song.
It doesn't matter if it's dead of winter
Or if the cold outside is nasty and bitter—
Still the kingly trees stand majestically in the ground;
To Mother Earth they are firmly bound.
Without their leafy foliage they stand in humiliation,
Until with warmer weather they quiver in anticipation.
They won't be skeletons forever—ugly and brown—
Soon, brilliant green will surround them like a crown.
The trees of winter are a thing of the past—
New growth, hues of spring—have come at last!

Patricia Jo Long
Terra Bella, CA

Family

It is so easy with words
to hurt someone else
words can be sharper than knives
and injure all their lives
There is nothing more important
In this life, but our families
We need to hold them close
And never make them cry
Hard to forgive when we are hurt
We keep dwelling on things said
until it becomes a mountain
It could stay till we are dead
Can't get over a mountain
Words said get in the path
Then they create hurt feelings
and stir someone's wrath
Don't we need to climb above it
to gain good will again
to love our family always
then, and only then we will win

Polly B. McElroy
Aberdeen, WA

The Playhouse

Why would you sit there pretending to drink tea
when you walked out on me so casually.
You sit there faceless like a porcelain vase trying to hold onto
your awkward teacup with fingers smelling of lies and deceit.
You try to utter words of devotion and innocence
as your words tangle together not knowing one truth from the other
as my ears have gone dead.
I used to wait for you in that house on Esslemont Road night after night
and all I heard was "Leave me alone, leave me alone."
I used to be your one and only as you did this
with your legs spread wide open
sitting there in your brown skirt, brown hat, and shoes.
Now we sit here together passing back and forth
make-believe scones and jam,
me asking you "How many sugars for your tea?"
But then again, Mother,
everything is just pretend here within this playhouse.
Guess you are, too.

Myraka Jones
The Villages, FL

Myraka Jones was born in England and moved to the United States in 1964. Having spent her formidable years in an English orphanage, Myraka's gift of poetic storytelling came to her early in life. As an escape from the indignities of her early childhood, she withdrew as her imagination grew. Myraka's poetry takes the reader on a soul-searching journey through words, thoughts, and questions she hopes many can relate to.

Pelican Cove

Palm trees swish in sultry air
The scent of citrus and you're aware
Pelican cove has a secret haze
Nestled on the gulf coast in a maze

A peacock cries like one in pain
Carried on the wind and subtle rain
He shows his fan in mock disdain
You are intruding in his domain

A grapefruit falls from a tree beyond
Softly bouncing on the spongy ground
This land was planned with futures in mind
To love the creations of all mankind

Better hurry don't be late
Shelling boat leaves right at eight
Island sands will toast your toes
Looking for the shells the waves dispose

Blossoms in splendor and colors to adore
Leaving us to ponder about life in store
The paradise of creature and plants abound
On the edge of the sea with tidal sounds

Charlotte C. McLaughlin
Lakewood, CO

No Tail Tale

The tale of no tail—
no (tail)ing how this tale started
or how it might end.
On the mockingbirds tail, the cat, and the wind.

Overheard it being said you could catch
a bird by putting salt on its tail.
Hmmm—let's ponder this.
Can I fly without my tail or will I just
go around in tumbling circles?
Will the wind catch my wings to keep me
aloft or will all be lost?

Maybe I should ponder this more before I pluck.
But if I don't, with salt I'll be caught
and caged never to fly again.
Wait! What's salt? And who puts it on my tail?

While in ponder I forgot to look.
Pounce came the cat and feathers popped out from
the root.
I can fly. I can sing. I can mock the cat
whose salt he did not bring.
What is salt anyway . . . No (tail)ing.

David Hayes
Woodland, CA

I grew in the 1950s outside a small town—Esparto, CA. My parents and grandparents were farmers. Growing up in a rural area you learn to entertain yourself and attune yourself with nature and serenity. Folklore and stories from elders always came into play and were cherished memories. And wives' tales could never be ruled out and always fascinated me. Hence, no tail tale. Remember, if you lose or pull a tooth and never stick your tongue into the empty socket, a gold tooth will appear!

Mending Each Silvery Cloud

Mending each silvery cloud
The gentle wind had tore
Holding the seams equally
To stitch them as before
Pieces seem irregular
Of those she never wore
Trimming holds by golden thread
Sunlight open its door
The wind blew her amber skirt
And left her half exposed
Shows her in all her glory
With very little clothes
Evening comes she dresses herself
In silky purple coat
Hurry on the other side
Where morning is promote

Barbara Singh
Woodhaven, NY

Magical Paradise

As we grow older,
I hope we don't lose the magic
of living and enjoying our wonderful Earth,
waking up hearing the melodious
singing of the birds outside on the
green tall trees as they move with
the rushing of the wind
while beautiful foaming white clouds
start sailing through the blue, blue sky,
slowly passing over the bright warm sun.
The sun sneaks through the clouds,
blazing with warm rays and
encircling all around us.
The wind caresses us all as it moves on,
taking our worries with it,
joining the beautiful butterflies
flying from flower to flower,
dancing with the wind as they move
with the rhythm of their wings.
The beautiful hummingbirds join them,
swishing their beautiful wings
back and forth, having so much fun
on this Earth's magical paradise.

Stella B. Angulo
Peoria, AZ

Back in the Day

The other day someone said,
Do you remember back in the day?
Before cell phones and computers
when families gathered together
around the dinner table.
Adults and children conversing
with each other with plenty to say.
Later children playing together,
adults chatting or with board games,
everyone laughing and shouting,
good times held by all.
Back in the day we enjoyed one another's
company with lots and lots of love to share.
Those were the good times
back in the day.

Darlene K. Lannholm
Galesburg, IL

Seeing families sitting together with phones in hand instead of talking with one another brought this to mind.

Another Ride

When we come through the darkness and come out on the other side
We may say, Thank you, God, or What a hell of a ride.
However you say it, just say it.
Whatever works for you will fit.
There's two sides to all things for us—maybe nine ways to skin a cat.
When we get beyond dualism, we'll know this is this and that is that.
We're all human with challenges to face; I face mine here,
you face yours in your place.
But, when all is said and done, none are excluded.
Anything can happen to anyone.
Our utmost hope as we travel our road is that there's strength within
to help us with our one-on-one while feeling the help of our friends.
So, as we grow older and get to know ourselves better,
hoping this helps to deal with stormy weather.
We know as we move on, enjoying life with less ego and pride,
it will only be a matter of time before there's another ride.
While we ride the roller coaster or maybe a seesaw
make the most of your life as you ride, y'all!

Sherry York
Arab, AL

The Thunder Road

Forevermore the moon
Brightens the darkened sky
Shines on starry nights
As stars fly by
The flame that fires the soul
Where can it be
When it is but an ember
Of time long ago
In each and every heart
There are secrets loosely kept
Under the rugs of our minds are they swept
Sail away in a dimension of desire
And chase the wind till it fans the fire
The light of day bounces off
Walls of thunder
And echoes a language
Heard among the stars
The road to thunder is no wider
Than the window of clear emotion
Or cloudy illusion
But roads are meant to be traveled
Even as life is meant to be lived

George Benaquista
Belleville, NJ

I love all forms of art such as music, painting, poetry, and sculpture. I am fascinated by the talent of artists. What inspired me to write this poem was the hardship I experience in life and the spark of imagination that flows from my mind.

Do You Know?

Do you know where you're going to,
Or do you like what life is showing you?
Do you know Jesus as your Lord,
Or are you living of your own accord?
Do you know the blessing and pardon you receive,
Or are you afraid to come to Him and believe?
Do you know it's not too late,
You can come to Him and change your fate?
Jesus will save your soul from hell;
He'll teach you to live well.

Shannon Young
Jacksonville, AR

Renaissance

From Genghis Khan to Ghandi
From Caligula to Jesus
Tides of willful dominance
Ebb with restless submission
Renaissance rises on occasion
Only to restart this folly
Outrage, aggression, jealousy
How to stop this cycling
Tides of starry genius to thuggery
Fulfill the deepest joys of life
Laughter, toys, and curiosities
Because we all are children

Camille Einoder
Chicago, IL

The Family Tree

I am the little girl
smiling in an old family picture
that's hidden in a shoebox
in the hall closet.

I am from a small town
where trains do not stop
and the road ends.
I am from the soil
that grows the garden
that feeds the family.
I am from the rose
that blooms outside my window
and from the cherry trees.
I am part of the forest
that covers the mountains
and sustains life.
I am the promise
of unfulfilled dreams
and renewed hope.

I am the little girl
smiling in an old family picture.
I am but one leaf
on the family tree.

Nancy E. Tayman
Akron, OH

Listen, Can You Hear What I Hear?

Listen, really listen, can you hear it?
The thundering of the rain as it hits
The howling of the wind crashing by
If you listen it speaks to you.

Listen, really listen, can you hear it?
The thrashing and screaming of forest animals running
The howling of the crackling forest fires
If you listen, it speaks to you.

Listen, really listen, can you hear it?
The scuffling of worn shoes of rejection
The desperate sigh of a father looking for work
If you listen, it speaks to you.

Listen, really listen, can you hear it?
The crying of lost babies
The mourning of immigrant mothers
If you listen, it speaks to you.

Listen, really listen, can you hear it?
The whimpering of children hiding under a desk
The popping sounds of guns going off in the school hall
If you listen, it speaks to you.

Listen, really listen, can you hear it?
The marching, the protesting, the rallies, the gatherings
The cry for us to come together as one against hate
If you listen, it speaks to you.

Jeannie Sieck
Toledo, IA

Mother's Loving Hands

As a child I ran and played
with my brothers and friends,
but when I needed a gentle touch
I turned to Mother's loving hands.

So often my teen years were marred
by disappointments and fears;
during those trying moments
Mother's loving hands wiped away the tears.

As a young man I traveled
around the world again and again;
it was always great to come home
and feel the touch of Mother's loving hands.

As the years slowly passed
Mother's life altered my plans,
but I still cherish the touch
of Mother's loving hands.

Carl Sellards
Beckley, WV

Index of Poets

A

Akian, Rosemarie 90
Alcaraz, Alexandra Rose 53
Allen, Tina 122
Angulo, Stella B. 330
Arnold, Amanda Patricia 85
Ashker, Rich 283
Aukerman, Robert B. 185

B

Backalenick, Irene 1
Bailey, Corinne 265
Bajsarowycz, Lynette 158
Bakhos, Friday 221
Bangert, Gordon 297
Banner, Cole 136
Barnes, Ethelyn 306
Bass, Jane F. 186
Battle, Geisha 7
Beach, Margaret 30
Beauchamp-Boettger, Alisha 197
Begeer, Sandra 35
Belensky, Marie E. 94
Belland, Joel B. 7
Belokosa, Bozana 240
Benaquista, George 333
Bennett, Lorenzo 290
Benson, Paul Stephen 183
Bessler, William P. 305
Blagrove, Pauline Eurica 49
Blake, Gabrielle 284
Blakeny, Eleanor 194
Bloom, Rose 260
Boal, B. J. 10
Bogle, Vernon 149
Bonacci, Bernadette 156
Bortz, Chrissy 159
Bowden, Alexis 233
Bowlin, Denise E. 173
Bowman, Virginia 5
Branson, Martha Bond 221
Bresko, Christel Decker 119
Brett, Fay 208
Brewer, Carol D. 110
Brinkman, James Fred 150
Broussard, Catherine Johnson 91
Brown, Jacob E. 178
Brown, Victor 118
Brugler, Ruth E. 57
Bryant, James H., Jr. 225
Buczek, Joe E. 175
Burns, Rebecca 293
Byrnes, Pauline 282

C

Cambilargiu, Joh 237
Camp, Frances Elaine 148
Camp, Jack 307
Carberry, Marshelle 280
Carden, Rhonda R. 45
Cardwell, Sonia 307
Carl, Neal A. 256
Carlton, Carrie 83
Casale, Julia Rose 153
Catching, David 248
Cennami, Judy 217
Chandler, Bernice 291
Chau, Hanh N. 239
Chazan, Sharon 134
Clanton, Teresa 291
Cocina, Roberto 210
Collins, Irma H. 317
Collins, Julius 140
Collins, Scarlet 18
Colterelli, Theodore P. 249
Combs, Kenneth L. 82

Cook, Char Marie 287
Costa, Lesa 63
Councilman, Carolyn 312
Cox, Doris 13
Cox, Nancy L. 215
Crede, Barbara 315
Culver, Bonnie 98
Curtis, Chevelyn 80

D

Danes, Renee 272
Dawson, Hallette C. 238
Deaton, Victoria Elise 137
Dellolacono, Janice J. 16
DeLorenzo, Mariah 46
Dingus, Dollie 32
Djaniants, Anush 313
Donnelly, Kathleen Rose 60
Donner, Neal 263
Dorsey, Stanley Robert 304
Drebes, Roberta E. 321

E

Einoder, Camille 334
Elkins, Alfred 17
Elmer, Corena M. 38
Epps, Jessie 286
Espinoza, Joe J. 121
Evans, Dianne T. 6
Evans, Kayla 188
Evans, Sheila 156
Ezzell, Catherine A. 241

F

Faschingbauer, Loraine 66
Fellers, Lisa 269
Flemming, Malachi 275
Forstner, Kathleen 126
Foss, William R. 261
Frazier, Mildred E. 118

Freeman, Jerry T. 285
Freeman, Sharon Etta 222

G

Gaines, Alma M. 40
Garrett, Ginger 86
Georgick, Lily 146
Gervin, Mary A. 263
Gill, Lowell Grant 105
Gish, Debra L. 182
Goldfarb, Marvin D. 22
Goldstein, Lois A. 25
Goldworth, Nina 170
Gorman, Marianne 218
Graham-Gilreath, Ladyann 180
Granello, Jo Ann 229
Grantham, Betty Paschall 166
Graziaplena, Louis M. 19
Greathouse, Rosemarr 124
Greco, Rita 309
Gregg, Pat 166
Gross, Helga 193
Grube, Dean C. 135
Guerra, Victoria Nichole 76
Guiney, Mable M. 51
Guran, Aida Maria 69
Gushea, Dee 164

H

Hagwood, Earline 29
Hale, Amy Allen 37
Hannawell, Vickie 164
Hardel, Maricel 150
Harville, Maxine 58
Harwood, James 243
Hattendorf, Cecilia 259
Hayes, David 328
Hayes, Walker 71
Heggem, Nancy J. 234
Heim, Charlene K. 114
Heineman, Carol M. 127
Hemmen, Richard P. 50
Herbert, Jean B. 219

Hetherly, Jan L. 12
Hildebrand, Ellen E. 116
Hill, Lisa 203
Hitzemann, Marvin 79
Holmberg, Glynn 107
Holt, Connie R. 115
Honis, Ronald E., Jr. 60
Hotti, Angelica 286
Hovik, Douglas 230
Howard, Vonda 55
Howe, Juliet Grinnell 102
Howland, Laurie 64
Hudson, Joyce 128
Huie-Jolly, Mary Rebecca 169
Humphries, Madison 192

I

Ingrassia, Shaunna M. 295
Irwin, William D. 3

J

Jackson, Inez 271
James, Mae Nell 196
Jen, Alyx 2
Johnson, Curtis R. 178
Johnson, Debra Kay 316
Jones, Myraka 326
Jordan, Lauren Elizabeth 268

K

Kallas, Katherine 172
Kapa, Mike P. 261
Kaplan, Virginia L. 123
Keedy, Joyce 138
Keifer, Laura M. 251
Keith, Helen-Anne 4
Kelly, Empress 111
Kelsey, Olivia S. 131
Kempf, Joseph H. 189
Kennedy, Melissa 81
Kibbe, Heidi Marie 252

King, Betty L. 298
King, David P. 104
King-Jeffers, Sharon W. 43
King, Roberta A. 78
Knudsen, Linda J. 42
Knutson, Ann Lee 232
Kraft, Daniel P. 48
Kukula-Briggs, Dante 103
Kumar, Tanvi 162
Kus, Michiko Tokunaga 139

L

Lambert, Steven M. 96
Lannholm, Darlene K. 331
Leckbee, Christine M. 322
Liagouris, Constantine 206
Liebl, Susan Elizabeth 308
Litschewski, Sandi 323
Lladoc, Letitia M. 224
Long, Patricia Jo 324
Lorilla, Adelfa G. 11
Lotzer-Smith, Jennifer Ann 252
Lovenduski, Adrian J. 168
Love, Winifred J. 212
Lumpkins, Lee 245

M

Mann, Ruth Marie 298
Margarete, Joelle 213
Mariner, Latitia 41
Martinez, Daphne 44
Matros, Ron 17
Mayhugh, Shayla 142
McCoy, Virginia 4
McCulla, Hazel Lynn 296
McElroy, Polly B. 325
McGarvey, Martin P. 171
McKee, B. J. 237
McLaughlin, Charlotte C. 327
Melet, Robin Lynne 132
Melia, Holly 13
Mendrick, Stan A. 88
Meney, Vera M. 231

Meno, Julia M. 101
Mitchell, Donna M. 154
Mitchell, Wayne 236
Monteiro, Darryl 213
Morales, Oriana 151
Morales, Serenity 262
Morrow, Milton E. 187
Murphy, Jefferson 222

N

Naber, Karen S. 21
Needlman, Rhoda 89
Neubauer, Marlene 310
Newberry, Wayne 91
Nguyen, Minh-Vien 245
Nogales, Juan R. 39

O

O'Brien, Arvel E., Jr. 65
O'Kelley, Shannon L. 144
Olivas, PJ 49
Olsen, Braden 31
Orban, Toni Jo 27
Ott, David A. 214
Owen, Edith 61

P

Page, Barbara L. 87
Palma, Cinthia J. 264
Paulsen, Laura L. 257
Pearce, Margaret Coralie 273
Peat, Ron 204
Pederson, Lu Ann 260
Peña-López, Mary Alice 184
Pennella, Margo 23
Peretti, Peter O. 56
Peterson, Marilyn 174
Petrina, Heather 300
Phillips, Helon 216
Pourmehr, Mitra 141
Powell, Westley Louis, Jr. 8

Priestley, Benita Lashae 212
Puls, Shay 276

R

Ray, Breanna 73
Reinhart, Amber Sue 155
Richter, Frances 106
Rizo, Milagros 163
Roach, Rebecca M. 211
Roberts, Wilbert 70
Robinson, Dane L. 152
Robinson, Nickole Caryn 207
Rodriguez, Charles 72
Roe, Carsen 235
Rogers, Anita 14
Rootes, Neva P. 267
Roper, Carol Welty 244
Ruml, Sarah Elizabeth 288
Russell, Harry J. 223
Russell, Saundra 187
Russom, Debra 200

S

Sabiston, Larry 289
Sadler, Judy-Suzanne 279
Sadler, W. V. 195
Safko, Dorothy 67
Saiz, Frances 316
Salmon, Leanora 226
Sanchez, Ipolita 133
Sanders, Virginia 143
Santos, Laura 278
Sarkozi, Brittany 299
Scarborough, Sheryn 318
Schmidt, David M. 318
Schomberg, Carl Arthur 247
Scott, Sawyer Emily 33
Sellards, Carl 337
Sells, Clinton 190
Shackleford, JoAnn 113
Shaver, Donna J. 47
Shaw, Jennifer M. 167
Shaw, Jill J. 209

Sherlock, Monica 199
Shifflett, Wilma Lee 130
Sieck, Jeannie 336
Simmons, Esther Grace 303
Singh, Barbara 329
Singh, Sushant K. 177
Slisz, Candace M. 36
Slurzberg, Yaffa Erica 242
Smith, Catherine 183
Smith, Janice 246
Smith, Jeannie C. 101
Smith, Laura P. 220
Smith, Roy A. 28
Smith, Virgilia A. 9
Solomon, Francis Dianne 92
Sonder, Meghan Elizabeth 99
Stakston, Becky 255
Steinbach, Enola J. 301
Stepsay, Richard 16
Stewart, Carole A. 294
Stone, Khoda L. 79
Stone, Sean C. 319
Stoyak, Stephanie 266
Stuart, Elizabeth Anne 314
Sumner, Cherie Leigh 52
Sundberg, Carl E. 109
Sustarsic, Carol A. 20
Swan, Kenneth 320

T

Takeshima-Price, Mieko 100
Taylor, Christopher 258
Taylor, Jewelean 75
Taylor-Keck, Jill 15
Taylor, Thomas A. 62
Tayman, Nancy E. 335
Tew, Margaret 202
Tharp, Cheri 97
Thielman, LeRoy F. 112
Thompson, Clay 95
Thompson, Elizabeth 171
Thompson, Marshall 250
Thornton, Judy 311
Tolbert, John Mark 59
Toliver, Debbie 241

Tovatt, Debra 160
Treadway, Brianna 129
Tucker, Bonnie F. 26
Twardowski, Ronald 77
Tyler, Phyllis 292
Tynes, Robbie 303

V

Valese, Daniel 24
Vaughn, Dottie A. 201
Vinson, Emauri 253
Voyles, Hannie J. 50

W

Wahl, Gavin J. 181
Wallace, Myles 93
Waller, Ruby Zandra 176
Walsh, Donna 28
Walthing, Claudia 147
Ward, Austin 270
Wasinger, Jake 302
Watkins, Ezekiel J. 198
Weaver, Emberly Rose 281
Weidner, Trish Ellen 161
Weller, Martha 179
Whitaker, Corinne 108
White, Penelope H. 165
White, Shannon 205
Whitley, Ralph 228
Wik, Timothy A. 68
Wilke, Tess J. 74
Williams, Chester 181
Wilson, Helen 145
Wilson, Julian Alwyn 277
Winter, Marilyn 274
Witucki, Kimberli 254
Wolfschmidt, Willi 84
Worley, Margaret 120
Worthy, Charles 36
Wright, Maggi 117

Y

Yates, Jerry 227
Yeck, Joan Patterson 75
Yohn, Pamela J. 191
York, Sherry 332
Young-Lionshows, Alice Marie 54
Young, Nelson F. 157
Young, Shannon 334

Z

Zoë, Shalom Christina 125
Zoller, Ollie V. 34